This book is dedicated to
the costume & cosplay
community:
across all
ages, ethnicities, genders,
religions & orientations.

Our diversity is our strength.

The Halloween Collection:
Costume & Cosplay Techniques

was made possible thanks to the support of these lovely people:

Brandon
Andy K.
Roxanne Dobbs
Vulpecula
Craig Hackl
Kathy K.
Daniel and Jessica Featherstone
Rachelle LeeAnn Harkey
Bonsart Bokel
Crisolite
Alex Fullerton
Neal Hill
Rolf & Lynda Herzog
Joey Nirschl
M.T. Hall
Kate Peterson
Jesse Nystrom
Vicki Hsu
Karen Berquist Dezoma
Mary Hicks
Jennifer Fordham
Aelf
Michelle Cheever
Madison Knabe
Emily Hein
Nora Mai
Superstar Sissypants
Thax
De Lan
Squid Widget
Connie Janda
Bonnie Stewart

Nanna L.S.
Morgan Gordon
Michelle Kiscaden
Mike & Kristen
Mel & Jeff
Lina
Steve Hayes
Natalya Evangeline
Violet Amelio
Katerina Stappas
Mini Opalewski
Becky & Mark
Becky Benishek
Lauren Zawilenski
Mary Prince
Victoria Heckman
Maiden Muffin
Emerson S. Vranich
Professor Suffering Bastard and His Paramour, Allotta Colada
Rita Allen
Nick Brattoli
Janine Marie
Ansel and Tabitha Burch
Sheryl Woods
Jean Kveberg
Julie Cudahy
Ann
Maria Davies
Alan Vuchachevich
Eric Fettig

Ken Amelio
C. Dearing
Cassie and Jerry Beyer
Linda and Glenn Meyer
Jason R. Merril
Christopher Poletto
Ivy Klynge
Katie French
Julianne Hunter
Kai Borsecnik
Mick Gall
Vida Cruz-Borja
Ann Peru Knabe
James Weigel
Marie
Captain Sam Perkins-Harbin
Lyndzi Miller
Amanda Price
Lilyana G.
Batzoro
Loren Morris
Rebecca R.

Pookie

Cover photograph by: Robert Remme

The Halloween Collection: Costume & Cosplay Techniques

Written by
Laura Meyer

Photography by:
Laura Meyer
Robert Remme
Kate Peterson

Published by
Twilight Ember Education Services LLC

Hardcover ISBN: 978-1-458042-02-1

First printing in March 2025
Printed in the United States of America

Foreword

I'm writing this a year later than I had planned. It is my habit that the foreword of a book is the absolute last thing that I do before sending it to the printer, so that you can… enjoy?… my up-to-the-minute experience. And the last year was rough… I heard from friends and read numerous articles online that it was a particularly rough one for folks trying to make a living in creative fields. This is partly because rising costs across the board have forced us all to consider non-essential purchases carefully, and the arts are often considered non-essential.

So I would like to take this moment to express my appreciation to you for purchasing this book, and especially to all the amazing folks who backed the kickstarter to fund the first printing of this book; they had the faith in me to put their hard-earned towards this endeavor, and it couldn't have happened without them.

For my part, the last year felt like I was running from deadline to deadline, trying to catch my breath. Fortunately, I have a very rewarding part-time job with a wonderful company that does great work in helping folks with varying levels of disabilities become more independent in their everyday lives. So I wasn't left short on rent, or needing to abandon my small business, as so many in our country have. Over the last handful of months, working towards the completion of the writing, the photographs, and the layout (I design my own books in InDesign because I am insane) has been a type of therapy- a feeling of accomplishment at a time when so many of us feel we have little control over what is going on in our world.

"The Halloween Collection: Costume & Cosplay Techniques", is nearly 40 pages longer than my first book. As difficult as that is to believe, it contains the same number of chapters. But there was so much more to dig into in this book. Book one was very focused; specific sewing techniques I used on specific gowns, with lovely pictures. I received a lot of feedback on my first book, mostly very positive. Many people commented on how beautiful and professional the final product was, and on how much information it contained. But I paid attention to the critiques as well- there were many people who wished I covered more than sewing, and included more than just gowns. There was also some silly criticism; one person did not read anything about the book and was then displeased that it was not about antique Victorian clothing. "Not very exciting," was one book review, making me wonder if I should have added a car chase somewhere in there.

Well there are no car chases in my second book, but the chapters are longer because you will find more costumes and so much more than sewing and lovely dresses!

IV

Whether you're a master foam-smith, professional costumer, or you have just begun delving into costuming or putting together your own cosplays, you will find something useful in this book. Take a look at the table of contents to get a hint... multiple skillsets, across multiple costumes in every chapter.

As hard as it is for us to admit, we can't be masters at everything when we're first learning new skills... but my goal is to give you the means of shortening your learning curve. I want to help make that first project with fabric painting, or wigs, or 3D printed parts, as successful as it can possibly be....
and to do it in a fun way, with groan-worthy puns and honest recountings of my own experiences, both the successes and the tough lessons.

I am laying bare a shared vulnerability in this book, exposing my soft underbelly to you. Because, like you, I want my project to be successful. I want my costume to look GOOD. And I don't enjoy not knowing that new skill, or fumbling around with that new material.
But I give you all of it- what I'm happy with as well as what I still need to work on. And I'm still learning.

The unique feature of this book that I'm terribly proud of having thought of is the "Expert's Corner". Since I am relating my learning experiences with new costuming skillsets and techniques, I thought it would be valuable to still offer professional, expert advice in some of these areas. So I recruited industry professionals and renowned designers and costumers to offer their insight to you. FIVE experts, covering latex prosthetics, wigs and headpieces, leatherworking projects, dyeing fabric, and the preparation and painting/weathering of 3D printed parts.

In the meanwhile, I have also just designed a costume/cosplay journal, to chronicle the creative journey of other makers, and I am working on finishing the murder mystery game "Cogs Aplenty" for 2025. I have a ballgown to finish and I've just begun planning my next cosplay, but I'll be writing again soon and my next book could take us in a couple different directions; history, erotica, or another costuming book that I know I have in me. You're welcome to join me on any or all of these literary adventures!

I hope you enjoy this book and as you go forward, remember that everyone is at a different place in their journey. One of the things that makes the costuming/cosplay community so special is the unbridled enthusiasm and support so many of us have for everyone's creativity. So get out there, get creative and have fun!

Laura Meyer

Contents

Facing Page Models: Richard Kern, Mica Chenault
Photographer: Kate Peterson

Photographer: Robert Remme

Chapter One

Make It Your OWN Instead of Making It YOURSELF
Customizing Purchased Costumes

"There's no need to reinvent the wheel."
This mantra guided me, and seemed like the perfect way to begin my second book on costuming.

After all, every year we see more comic or hero-focused movies and shows, and more conventions pop up every year appealing to a range of cosplay genres.
The prevalence of online shopping and a worldwide marketplace has made it easier than ever to find, and order, pre-made costumes as new characters are introduced to pop culture. You may ask yourself, should I buy it, or should I attempt to make it?

Your Reasons May Vary
The reasons to buy a premade costume are simple:
You may lack the time, desire, construction skills, or funds to make the costume yourself... or any combination of the above. You may decide to make one part of the costume, but not all of it. Or you may be choosing to focus on just making the armor or a prop for a particular costume build.
Whatever the reason, chances are that the purchased costume will not arrive as a perfect fit, and you'll want to make adjustments to it.
This chapter may assist you in tackling some common types of alterations and modifications.

Buckle in, because I packed a LOT of information into chapter 1!

Starting the book with this topic was meaningful to me because I've worked through some internal stigma surrounding purchased costumes.
At times I've thought "I can't enter this costume contest, I didn't make it myself!".

After I bought my Lady Dimitrescu (Resident Evil Village, 2021) costume I heard myself speak self-deprecatingly about purchasing it, and hurriedly listing the adjustments I made to it.

I have stepped back, reflected on my own views, and worked on breaking down the attitudes that were clearly there.
For chapter one of my second book, if I was going to talk the talk, I needed to walk the walk. So I'll be discussing, proudly, the two pre-made costumes I recently purchased and made adjustments to.

Besides Lady Dimitrescu (Lady D), the other costume purchase I'll be discussing in this chapter is Captain Carter. The purchases saved me time, money, stress, and I still achieved a custom fit and an improvement on a number of details. How can *you* do the same? Let's get into it.

Step 1- Researching Options

The first step for both costumes was research. After examining images of the original outfit at all angles online, I visited the websites linked to dozens of images of the costume. I evaluated the websites for legitimacy, looked for a range of honest (not just five-star) reviews and searched for customer pictures attached to reviews.

Red Flag, Green Flag

I was on the lookout for websites that looked hastily put together, gaps in information like contact emails or phone numbers, a lack of any sort of return/exchange policy, and costumes with only one or two images.

Then I drilled down into details: did the website specify the materials or fabrics used? Are the images high quality? Do the costume details appear consistent from one image to the next? One way to weed out questionable sites is to actually contact them via phone or email with a simple question, like their estimated shipping time. If you get a timely, professional response that's a definite green flag!

"Lady D"
(if you can find a consensus on pronunciation, tell me)

I originally planned to make Lady D myself as a budget costume, sourcing the material from another dress or secondhand. After examining the details of the costume, I decided it would be unlikely to find a dress with enough fabric to make the gathered front panel from a resale store, and buying two dresses from a store (or enough fabric for the dress) would defeat the "budget" part of the plan.

#HatAttack

So I began online research for pre-made options. One dress was on a handful of sites, but was lacking in defining details and also appeared to have no stretch in the fabric from the way it fit the models in the images.

Another dress had some mixed reviews, with comments on the material being very stretchy, the dress being too long, and one comment that despite the material feeling thick it was somewhat see-through.

I looked more closely at this second option. This dress had accurate sleeve and shoulder drape details, and I considered the extra length as a bonus. Lady D is over 8 feet tall, and I planned to wear my highest

3

heels for the costume. If it was a little sheer, I could wear a slip under the dress. And a stretchy fabric meant more play with adjustments.

The dress came with gloves, a hat, a black flower and a faux pearl necklace, but I had already pulled a flower, gloves and necklace from my stash of accessories. As for Lady D's enormous black hat, I assumed the one that came with the dress would be awful and I sourced a BIG black straw beach hat online.

The Purchased Results
The length was great with heels on. The weight and stretch of the dress worked out well also. I did end up needing a full slip, which I pulled from my closet. I used the black flower the dress came with, and mine got to stay on the costume it was already attached to. The sad hat they included was, indeed, awful.

Lady Dimitrescu

The Alterations:
What I Did to Make it My Own
The stretch in the costume was really the best part, and I was happily surprised at how heavy the fabric was for an online purchase. I made the sleeves more fitted along my forearms. Since there was extra sleeve length, I used a heavy (upholstery or quilting) thread to stitch up a few inches along the outside of my wrist, and knotted the thread to create a gather. A few faux pearls (from the included necklace) were added along the gathers. I did a similar light gathering down the center back, and added pearls there too. In stills from the game the dress appears to button down the back with pearl buttons, but the stretch of fabric made this unnecessary, so mine are decorative.

The very broad-brimmed black hat I bought was reinforced with an immense amount of starch spray to lend a helping hand to a wire along the outer edge.
And with some curled hair and makeup I was set! A future addition may include the looong black claws she brings out when she's angry, but I was vending, so I needed to use my phone (and hands) for this event.

Captain Carter
I have two or three relatively easy (think "low time commitment" for getting ready, and high comfort level) cosplays to fall back on for

Thursdays or Sundays at cons. I had considered adding Peggy Carter to the list for a while. I have the right hair color, I can rock a vintage look… I even have dresses that could pass for being pulled straight from the racks of "Agent Carter". For some reason, though, the need for Agent Carter was never urgent. Plus, I have a Carmen Sandiego costume that hits a lovely nostalgic button for folks, and also works on a low-effort day.

But then Hayley Atwell took the stage as Captain Carter in "Dr. Strange and the Multiverse", and I was downright enamored. The idea of a Captain cosplay began noodling around in my brain.

A Need Out of Time

Her appearance again, in "What If", sealed the deal for me. In addition to my previous interest in cosplaying Carter, I had been regularly lifting the last couple of years, and really related to this particularly buff version of Peggy. However, this strong cosplay desire came at a particularly busy time for me. So I examined the costume, priced out the fabric preliminarily and roughly estimated the time to build it. Then I went through my online research process and evaluated the best option I found, compared to the cost and time it would take me to make it.

Yep, a Captain Carter cost-benefit analysis.

I determined that I would spend more on the fabric alone, and given my current schedule it would likely take several months to complete it once I was able to start it, and it was just as likely that it would sit partly done for months, instilling guilt every time I saw it, until the cosplay was barely relevant any longer. Whew!
So I just bought it.

Pre-Packaged Challenges

Modifying purchased costumes can actually be just as challenging in some ways as creating one from scratch. It's true! When making a costume, you have full control of your materials. With pre-made items, you need to work with what you're given. Even if the costume is decent quality, it may not be the material you would have chosen, or could present specific issues.
For example, the Captain Carter long-sleeved shirt with the "abs" is made from a material that snags on EVERYTHING. If you look at it funny, it snags. Out of spite. Also, the zippers were of extraordinarily weak construction. But overall, this particular costume had a lot of extra touches and details that most did not, and they were easy to see in the many detailed images online.

The Purchased Results

I was actually impressed by the level of detail, and the little extras that were put into this costume out of the box. I did go a size up

from my usual, since I have some Captain Carter Quads, and I couldn't pin down whether the fiber content included stretch. It ended up being the right call; it's always easier to make something smaller than it is to add size. Particularly because mass produced clothing rarely includes much of a seam allowance. The thighs and upper arms were roomy enough, and I had more than enough space everywhere else. The costume came with a pair of thrice-buckled strips on a slab of pleather that was meant to be a boot cover of some sort, and was the only thing that was a little perplexing. It also included the long-sleeved "abs" shirt, the cropped vest, the high-waisted pants, fingerless gloves, arm bracers, shoulder straps, and the belt with pouches.

The Alterations: What I Did to Make it My Own

As mentioned, I replaced the zippers on both the shirt and the vest. I took the waist in by several inches on both as well. To help the "abs" on the shirt lay flat, I added "V" of elastic at the bottom of the shirt in front and in back, and added snaps, effectively making it a bodysuit.

I was able to get in and out of it with just the zipper up the back, but even Captain Carter appreciates not having to fully undress to use the bathroom.

The pants were.... an adventure. Even by the 1940's "high-pants fast-talk" standards, these were *really* high-waisted.
I took the waistband off, removed about 1.75" from the top of the pants (with a little angling in at the back seam to reduce gapping) and put the waistband back on. I also tapered the pants and put in elastic to create stirrup bottoms, so they wouldn't ride up. The last adjustment

Captain Carter's yearbook photo

on the pieces I received was moving the velcro on the bracers over, so they weren't so big. Beyond that, I picked up a pair of brown leather gloves, as the fingerless gloves were uncomfortable after 3 minutes. I also took a pair of boots from the resale store, cut them down, and sewed the boot-cover-slabs over the tops.

Trust me, it looks much more orderly than it sounds.

To Bone or Not to Bone, That is the Question

"Boning" (not that, ya perv) is a strip of rigid material used for reinforcement in clothing, most commonly and historically in corsets.

Nearly everyone can go online (or to a store) and find plastic sew-through boning or plastic-coated steel boning in different lengths, and either boning channels or 1" wide bias tape with a simple search.

The issue of what boning to use and how to insert it is the larger question. Steel boning: usually treated or painted to avoid rusting, steel retains its shape reliably. It should be well-encased to be sure it doesn't work its way out through your fabric.

Plastic boning: Available in sew-through styles, it can be easier to use and more comfortable. However, it can lose its shape when warmed by body heat (giving an unflattering silhouette), and cut plastic edges can also work their way through fabric and be uncomfortable.

There are a few situations you may run into: Your clothing item may have two layers of fabric. In that case, you could sew two rows of stitches to make a channel where you want the reinforcement, inserting the boning into the channel. Be sure to close the top and bottom of the channel well.

Your item may have boning that you want to replace or upgrade. In that case, open the top of the existing boning channel, remove and

replace the old bones with the new one, and close off the top well.

The last possibility is that your costume item needs to have a channel placed for the boning to be put into. This is when you would use the boning channel or bias tape or twill tape, which would function as a boning channel). In this case, mark out the places you want to reinforce your costume piece and lay the channel down, pinning it in place. You will sew a line down the right edge of the channel, then another line up the left edge of the channel.

Be sure the channel you sew is wide enough for your metal or plastic bones to fit in! Keeping your stitching speed slow will make it easier to keep the stitching even.

Your Checkout Checklist
Online:
- **Website Legitimacy:** Does the website look established? Are there errors or misspellings? Urgency traps like "only two left!" or "sale ending soon!"? You can use website checkers like urlvoid.com to see if it has been flagged for malicious behavior, or just search the site name to see if others have had bad experiences.
- **The Costume Itself:** Are there multiple views of the item? Close-ups of details or fabrics? Can you see reviews for the costume? Check their size charts, or measurements for the costume item. More details are a green flag.

- **The Fine Print:** Check to make sure there are policies on the site for returns, payment, and customer support. Read them to make sure they make sense (I have seen places that say all items are eligible for return, but further down they say it's only if the package seal is unbroken.) Give their phone number, email address, or chat window a try to make sure they are active.

In-Person:
- **Give it a Try:** You should be able to try on the costume, or otherwise inspect it for quality. Move around in it some, as you expect to when wearing it at events- walk around, try sitting in it, etc. If there's a pose particular to the character, try it out in front of the mirror.

- **Returns:** There should still be a return policy and a means of contacting them with any issues. Be sure that you get a receipt that has this information, or that it's given with the receipt.

Chapter One Model: Laura Meyer
Captain Carter Photographer: Robert Remme

Chapter Two

Get to the Source
New and Used Fabrics

So you've decided to make your own costume, or the fabric part of it!

Perhaps the character you've chosen to cosplay is too obscure and not available online. Maybe you have a very specific vision for the execution of the look, or you are doing a mashup.

You may simply want the challenge of the build.

Or perhaps you feel the online costumes are too pricey.

Hopefully it's not the cost of the completed costume that has driven your decision, because there is a universal truth which all cosplayers and costumers know:

Fabric is expensive.

There are often gasps of horror, screams of shock and misery upon the initial visit to a fabric store, as once eager and wide-eyed creators are faced with rolls of fabric from $6 to $60 per yard. Okay, I'm exaggerating... about the screams.

In fact, nearly all materials are expensive. When you total all project material costs, including the costs of additional items you may need (trims, buttons, tools to set snaps or grommets, scissors, a sewing machine, etc) AND the time it will take you to create the costume, buying the completed costume is rarely more expensive than making it yourself.

It could be viewed as a challenge; the sourcing of discount fabrics, the borrowing of tools. And I am never one to shy away from a challenge. There *are* ways to mitigate the costs behind original creations, and in this chapter I will take you on a magical money-saving journey.

One of my favorite thrifty strategies is hitting up resale and vintage stores for unique buttons or unusual fabrics at a steal of a deal.

Queen of Resale

In fact, my first Game of Thrones costume was spurred by a thrift store find. Given my penchant for any evil queen costume, you would be forgiven for assuming that I went into that costume intentionally, but no. I was strolling the pre-loved racks, and happened to glimpse a rich red satin.

I fished out the hanger and discovered wide curling bands of gold embroidery along the bottom of each scarlet panel. I swiveled to my partner and brandished the satin, declaring, "I'm making a Cersei costume!!"

And so it was that my first Cersei dress was created from… curtains.

This was a wildly affordable costume. I made the crown from oven-bake clay. Cersei's metal corset belt was a collaboration with my husband, who used four pieces of aluminum sheeting, spare gold neck-lace chain and square medallions from an old metal belt I'd used for a Buttercup costume ages ago (which was thrifted). I bought a wig for less than $30, and that was more than I had spent on the rest of the pieces. Sometimes pieces just come together, and sometimes you can dig through your (or a friend's!) stash and find perfect additions.

Inappropriate Fabric? Me?!

Sourcing the right type of fabric for your project is also important. I had seen a beautiful toile design on a website which used the fabric for bedding and curtains. It was a black and white design featuring vintage Betty Page-style scenarios, and I absolutely had to make a dress from it.

Man, did I search. I looked high and low, and only once found a version that was purchasable by the yard. But it was PINK. Not acceptable. So I went back to the original website, and I calculated the best deal according to square footage and price, and bought 2 large shower curtains. It was a relatively thin cotton, not transparent but also not very sturdy.

When I made my Victorian style ball gown from it, I backed the fabric appropriately, but that doesn't keep the outside of the fabric from wearing down and staining more easily than it would if it was a better choice for the project. For me, it's worth the trade-off when people actually notice the pattern on this sweet, vintage-looking ensemble.

Hello There, Obi-Wan

Other times I've hunted, sometimes for years, until I found the perfect fabric Such was the case with my rendition of an Obi-Wan Kenobi costume. I used to preface that costume title with "genderbent", but realized when someone asked how it was genderbent and my answer was, "Because I'm wearing it," that there's essentially no difference in the creation of the classic jedi costume for a man, woman, Twi'lek, Asari, Klingon, etc.

11

Well, possibly the hood size on the outer robe for the Twi'lek.

Creating a costume inspired by Obi-Wan Kenobi not only allowed me to embody a beloved character but also gave me an opportunity to practice sustainability by utilizing thrifted fabrics. I had found a chenille throw to use for the tabard and backed it with a solid cotton. The inner tunic was made from a deliciously worn linen tablecloth (please see my cautionary tale below), and I found a braided leather belt which, attached to a wider leather strip, made a decent utility belt. I added some rivets, some cut off and spray-painted pens to serve as clip-on rations, and the base costume was nearly complete. Dark cotton pants were easy to find, as the waistband would be hidden under the tabard. Faux leather boots are an easy thrift store find (less so if you're an outlier in size ranges). But the robe eluded me.

I refused to pay $40-$50 per yard for a wool of the weight I would need. At long last, I came upon it- two heavy curtain panels, in the right brown and with a fantastic texture. As an extra bonus, it was already satin backed so I had no need to purchase more fabric for the lining. For those of you who enjoy a little fabric hunting, a jedi costume makes for a good starter, due to the absence of patterns and decorations on the fabrics, and the neutral color palette. The outer robe also makes it a great winter costume option!

Beware, or, BE Aware
And now the cautionary tale. Now, thrift stores can be treasure troves of unique fabrics and finds. When purchasing used fabrics, you are able to enjoy the visual and tactile benefits of washed and worn-in fabrics. A well-loved tablecloth will have the same comfort factor as an old pair of jeans. However (as I discovered with the linen tablecloth that became the inner tunic of the costume) it also greatly reduces the life of the fabric. The linen began breaking down at stress points, particularly under the arms and where I had it wrap-tied around the waist. It might look even more "authentic" to patch or mend it, but that wasn't what I had intended.

So when shopping, no matter how much you love your fabric discovery, try not to be blinded by NFE (New Fabric Energy). See it for what it really is rather than what you want it to be, and you'll save yourself heartache in the long run.

Sourcing Fabric

Online Tips:

- ***Simply Samples!*** If you are looking to buy fabric, most reputable retailers online(as well as brick and mortar stores) will supply samples for no or little cost. I definitely recommend this minimal investment to avoid massive disappointment when your fabric finally arrives… with unexpectedly little stretch, or of a much different weight than expected, or in a very different color than it appeared to be on your screen. A few samples will allow you to compare options and look at how secondary fabrics or trims work together.

- **Can I Throw It Back?** Check return policies! If you choose to purchase your yardage and find that you can't use it, having researched the return options on the site will save you cash AND a headache.

- **Extra, Extra!** Get a lil extra. Always, always get a little extra fabric. Even if everything goes according to plan and you make no mistakes and change your mind exactly never, you'll have a bit of leftover fabric with which to make a coordinating accessory or matching outfit for your squishmallow. Everyone wins

- **Clean Getaway:** Always wash before starting (anyone who has ordered from one of the big-box fast-fashion houses has probably had the following experience: Something arrives & looks fine, but gets washed and suddenly has no shape, is wrinkled, or has shrunk hopelessly, despite the care instructions being followed. It's called "sizing", it is in new fabrics, and it is why you want to wash your fabrics before using them in your costume creations. Admittedly, sometimes in the first example it IS because the care instructions for the cheap fabrics were not correct.)

Vintage/Used Tips:

- **Just One Condition:** Check the condition of the fabric- please refer to the Obi-Wan story above. Check and recheck the fabric over to ensure it will hold up for what you need.

- **Take Care!:** If it is new in the packaging (let's say you found 4 new sets of curtains with the perfect pattern for your costume) be sure to note the care instructions... it would be demoralizing to wash it for the first time and have it shrink/pucker/etc.

- **Enough is Enough:** Make sure you have enough. Redundant, but a worthwhile point, as you will NOT find that vintage/used fabric again.

More Vintage/Used Fabric Tips:

Cleaner than Clean: Always wash before starting. Familiar advice, from our "online tips", but the logic here is different from the reasoning behind washing new fabric. You don't know where it's been, how it's been worn/used, and you don't know what aromas (animal, body odor, perfumes) are going to be... activated by some body heat. Reusing fabric doesn't mean using dirty fabric, so be sure to wash it. You also don't know if there are lingering chemical substances of any kind on the fabric.

On the off chance that you REALLY want to keep a weathering or texture that you think wouldn't survive a laundering; first, consider how you will clean it going forward and second, give it a disinfecting with an appropriate commercially available spray OR a solution of vodka and water (1:4), a well-known cleanser in theater/costuming circles (also useful on dry-clean only clothing between washes).

Tips for Thrifting:

- ***Patience Is A... Be Patient:*** It may take time to find the right pieces. Visit multiple stores to increase your chances of finding suitable fabrics. Expand your search area.

- ***Collateral Damage:*** Just as with vintage finds, inspect fabrics for stains, tears, or other signs of wear. Minor imperfections can often be repaired, but significant ones may make a fabric unusable for your needs.

- ***Measure and Match:*** Bring a measuring tape to gauge the amount of fabric compared to what you need. Remember that you'll need different amounts of fabric if it is wider or less wide than standard bolts. As I've said before, whenever possible get more fabric than you think you'll need!

- ***On the Safer Side:*** Air-dry fabrics whenever possible to prevent shrinkage or damage from high heat, particularly if they do not have care instructions included/attached. If using a dryer, select a low heat setting.

Photographer: Robert Remme

Chapter 2 Cover Model: Katie French
Page 14 Model: Laura Meyer

Chapter Three

Film Inspiration
Reproduction or Interpretation?

Moving beyond *whether* you make your costume or not, is the question of *how* to make it. Particularly so when all your information on the costume begins and ends with pictures or stills from a film, show or comic.

Construction of a two-dimensional image into a wearable costume requires a unique sort of reverse-engineering + figural extrapolation skillset.
And if *that* sounds challenging, it gets even more so if you're working from comic or anime images of costumes that weren't necessarily drawn as wearable or realistic designs -or on realistic bodies- to begin with. (Hawk Girl, Nami, and Vampirella cosplayers feel this, among others!)

With cosplay events and conventions constantly popping up, and fandoms gaining traction in the mainstream consciousness, there are more resources available to the average costumer than there were twenty, or even ten, years ago.

There are now commercial patterns made after characters (e.g. pirates from Pirates of the Caribbean movies or characters from the series of films based on Tolkien novels), blogs/reels by others who created the same outfit or prop, groups established specifically to guide the creation of costumes at a certain standard (501st, I'm looking at you!). So many resources if you're cosplaying a mainstream character.

But if your cosplay is a comic character, non-human, from a vintage source, or in the more obscure or unknown realm, how do you even start developing an image into a craftable goal?

Before a three-dimensional creation can even be pictured, costumers and cosplayers often need to make a choice about *fidelity*; whether to keep the design as close to the source example as possible, or to make a "close enough" or even unique version of the costume. In other words, whether to make a faithful reproduction, or an interpretation.

In this chapter, I'll go over the versions I created of the charming Katrina van Tassel from "Sleepy Hollow", Mrs. Lovett from "Sweeney Todd, the Demon Barber of Fleet Street", and Obi-wan Kenobi from "The Phantom Menace"/"Attack of the Clones" era (as mentioned in chapter 2), with a different approach for each.

Katrina van Tassel

My reproduction of the striped dress worn by Katrina Van Tassel in Tim Burton's "Sleepy Hollow", made two (wow?!) decades ago, was more challenging due to the lack/unavailability of quality movie stills at the time. I watched the film closely, making my sketches and my notes, and then figured out the best ways to get the look I wanted.

I spent a long time looking for fabric. I needed a particular size black and white striped fabric, and "Pirates of the Caribbean" had not come out yet so pirate stripes were not quite as easy to find as they were for the decade afterward. I eventually found a heavy fabric on Ebay, in two large lengths, that was almost a denim weave. Looking back, I'm glad I got a fabric that heavy, as the costume is still holding up today.

The costume consists of a strapless, back lacing corset, a full-length skirt with two layers of ruffled trim at the hem, and a front closing jacket with a gathered bustle at the back. I handmade the pleated trim around the edge and sleeves of the jacket from the same fabric of the dress and length of sheer ribbon in white and in black. While the costume is certainly not a historically accurate early 1800's gown, its details are highly similar to the film version.

A little Lovett

Mrs. Lovett

Even a short five years later, the availability of movie stills made my interpretation of Mrs. Lovett from "Sweeney Todd: Demon Barber of Fleet Street" so much easier to create. For this costume, the challenge with working from these particular movie stills was that the lighting in most of the movie was very dim. The colors in the scenes were also highly desaturated. This was clear when viewing promotional shots, where the costume colors looked completely different at times. At that point, even if there were accurate pictures of the costumes from a textile exhibit, the question became, should it be accurate to the film, or to the reality of the existing costume?

It comes down to personal choice, as does nearly everything in costuming, and I chose to go with the feeling to the costume; a moody, desaturated version of Mrs. Lovett's bakery costume, when Sweeney Todd first walks into her establishment. Therefore I wasn't too concerned about making a structurally accurate late Victorian outfit, and focused on the

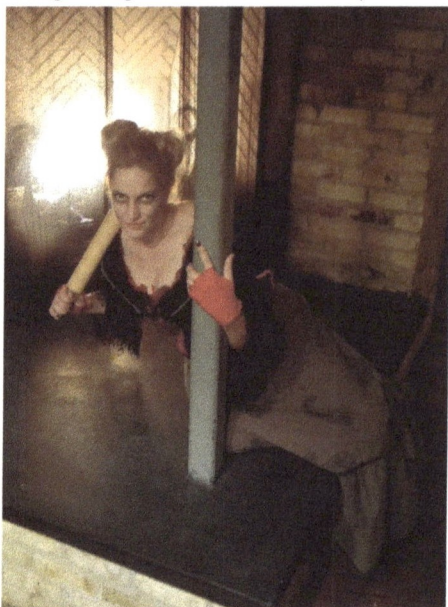

elements that made her costume stand out. I wanted to make a skirt with a bustle-inspired back. For both main characters, their monotones were really only broken by highlights of red. You can find more details on this costume, and the hand-painted design on the skirt, in chapter 8.

Bo-Buck

Developing your own visual interpretation of a character can be deeply satisfying and a fun experience! Mashups tend to be particularly creative costume interpretations, and they hold a special place for me in the cosplay world. There's nothing quite like seeing someone in a costume representing *two* of your beloved fandom faves, and you know they had to put that costume together themselves from the raw, insanely creative idea.

I've done a lot of historical inspired costumes, and I enjoy period cosplays, so sometimes I don't feel like I'm the most creative kid at the con. However, I had a great mashup idea, and it was a ton of fun! I was making a Bo Katan costume (see Chapters for details) and knew that I wouldn't be done with the armor in time for the convention at which I had hoped to wear it.

Inspiration!

First, I saw that Katee Sackhoff- the actress who portrays Bo Katan in "The Mandalorian" and also recently voiced the animated version of the character, was going to be at the convention as a celebrity guest!

Then, (super-sad background context here) I had the idea to do a couples costume with the partner I planned on being at the convention with. The idea was from a series that Katee had also starred in some years earlier, "Battlestar Galactica". As it turned out, dressing up as Starbuck and Lee Adama, the

onscreen poster children for dysfunctional relationships, would have been ironically appropriate. That relationship ended, as maintaining my dignity was more important than keeping it going, two weeks before the convention.

BUT THEN, I had the amazing idea to take my original idea and meld it with a better, independent version of Starbuck. Thus, Bo Buck was born, the unholy union of Mandalorian armor, pistols, and Starbuck's badassery.

I bought and modified the tank tops, holsters and wig. I bought the pants and dyed them darker (see chapter), and sewed on heavy velcro squares to adhere the 3D printed armor pieces to the legs more securely than the tied straps alone. After I bought a temporary tattoo was too small, I made a larger, accurate version and ordered a custom one. The final look came together really well. I've never bought

a celebrity photo op before, but I was really proud of my mashup. So I indulged, and it was fun; plus it seemed like she got a kick out of it.

Obi-Wan Kenobi

This costume's execution fell somewhere in between movie fidelity and interpretation. Really, it's a costume from a galaxy far, far away, and I'm not going to be passing for Ewan MacGregor anytime soon, so keeping strictly to a reproduction wasn't the goal. However, I *did* want it to be easily recognizable as a jedi costume to the average person, and identifiable as Obi-Wan to the average Star Wars nerd.

I focused on getting the visual details accurate rather than finding the same fabrics they used in the films. So I used chenille (a throw blanket!) for the tabard, which was a cotton gauze in the film, and I found a set of curtains that struck the perfect chord for the outer robe. Much cheaper than the fabric used in the movie, the weight and the movement of the fabric was just right.

The balance between historical accuracy and film or media-based fidelity is important in creating a believable costume, and you need to decide for yourself what your costume goals are for your project.

Where to start?

Study Those Images!

Cosplay Costume Journal:
From Concept to Convention

All-in-one planner to design, track and record 25 costumes

Perhaps a journal like this?

- **Devil, Details, Etc:** Note colors, fabrics, textures, and patterns. Beyond clothing, look at accessories, footwear, hair, and makeup. What about props or weapons? Sketch out your ideas, or start a collage for your costume in a notebook, or a cosplay journal.

- **Context Matters:** Consider the setting of the film, the character's role, and whether the character has any symbolic details that should be included.

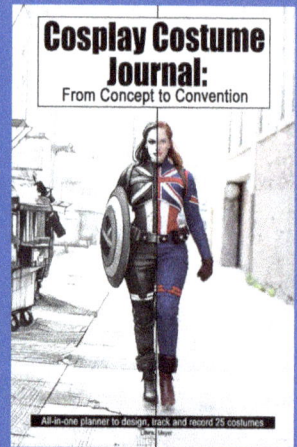

Do Your Own Research

- **Character:** Identify the personality, social class, and function of the character in the story. This can influence your choice of materials and overall design. (For example, Mrs. Lovett's costumes went from scraggly and dirty, to beaded extravagance due to her improved financial situation.)

- **Period!:** Take time to research the fashion/construction methods from the era of a period film/show. Reproduction or not; understanding how clothing was put together may help you with constructing your project!

- **Cultural Influence:** Think about the location or cultural context of the character's design. (For example, understanding or researching the Polynesian dress in "Moana")

Choose the Level of Accuracy That's Right for YOU

Historical Accuracy vs. Film Interpretation: Film costumes often take creative liberties (Bridgerton), incorporating modern fabrics, fantasy elements, or artistic interpretations of history. You could stay true to this design or incorporate period-correct historical details. There are many resources for period construction online, from video tutorials to instructional blogs.

Cosplay Considerations

- **Fan Adaptations:** If you're working solely from images, try to identify a base garment or pattern to start from. (For example, a long dress that could serve as a starting point for a Galadriel gown, or blue coveralls that you could add to for a vault dweller jumpsuit.)

- **Star Struck:** When creating a costume from a specific film or show, focus on the most recognizable elements of the costume (e.g., the stitching on Catwoman's bodysuit, One Piece's straw hat and red jacket, or the "M" on Mario's hat). These are necessities for your costume.

- **Keys, Phone, Wallet:** Key, identifiable accessories such as weapons, jewelry, or specific props can help a costume stand out and be recognized (Thor's cape and hammer, Mario's hat and moustache, Indiana's whip, the Joker's makeup). What do people instantly associate with the character? Be sure to include them in your plan!

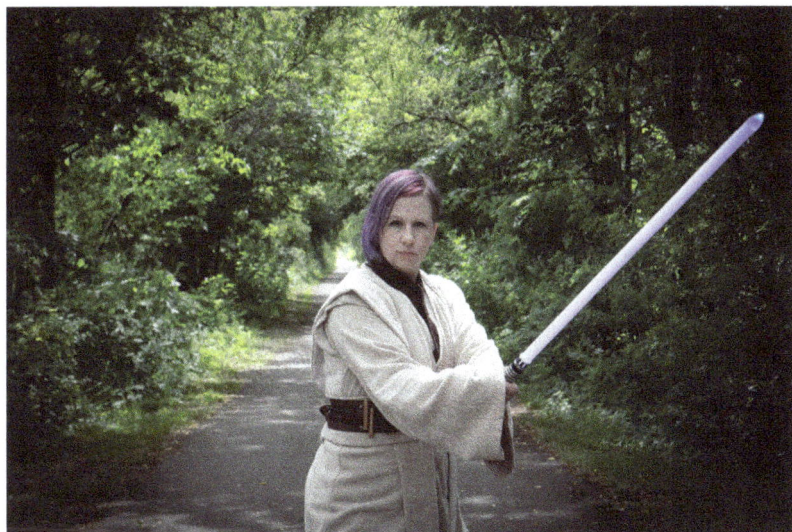

Model, above: Katie French
Photographer: Kate Peterson
Chapter 3 Cover Model: Becky Benishek

Chapter Four

Getting Overly Attached
Appliques, Patches and Cutouts

"Costume".

When I've thought of the word, I used to associate it with quality and endurance... or the lack thereof.

This is an inaccurate association that *can* be true, but is certainly not true all, or even most, of the time; many costumes I see at FanExpo, Teslacon, C2E2, etc., are well thought out and executed across a wide range of sewing, crafting and tailoring skill levels.

So I've reassessed my view of "costumes", and cosplays, over the years.

Now when I talk about "costumes" I'm making, it's usually a version of a character's outfit, and I'm not worrying about fiber content, historical accuracy in technique or (in some situations) finishing techniques.

All this to say...
it had been a long time since I had made a "costume" when I began my Cersei and Jaime Lannister costumes for Halloween in the early years of the Game of Thrones frenzy. I thought that, as far as a couple's costume goes, it was just the right amount of wrong. And I'll start by proudly stating that 90% of the fabric and "armor" was from thrift stores (see chapter 2 for more on that) and dollar stores.

This chapter will go over creation and attachment techniques for- you guessed it -appliques, patches and cutouts. Though it can seem intimidating, these techniques can add a lot to a costume!

For Cersei there were a wide range of looks to choose from, but I wasn't interested in one of her structured, wide 1950's style necklines, and I also didn't want to try to create her decorative, sculpted body armor. An early and frequently seen Cersei was in a red gown heavily embroidered at the neckline and sleeves, and the Lannister lion embroidered on hip gores of gold fabric. With a wide metal and maille belt, the look is regal and still possibly comfortable.

A McCall's pattern, 6940, obtained during a $1 sale functioned as a starting point. As you read in Chapter 2, I made a fantastic fabric find at a resale store, and I supplemented that with a gold silky fabric I had in my stash.

I made few adjustments to the pattern. The hip gore needed to be higher for accuracy and I raised the armscye for added mobility. I shortened the sleeves- a necessity due to a shortage of embroidered fabric. This is one negative side effect of thrifting your supplies; you have to face the fact that you work with what you've got, and there is no more available if you screw up. (No pressure though.) That's why my oft-repeated mantra in Chapter 2 was "always get a lil extra fabric!"

I *did* up finding more curtains, dark red sheers with gold embroidery that were a close match in color and style to the sleeve embroidery. Lucky find, honestly.

The Lion's Share… of Work

The coup de grâce, and the focus of this chapter, was the (Lannister) lion embroidered on the hip appliques. There was no way I was going to find lion appliques in the correct color and size, so I knew I would have to make them from scratch.

This was a process… I found an image (right) of a lion that was similar. Then I lengthened, narrowed and enlarged the image, estimating an appropriate size. It ended up being about 20 x 8 inches. I divided the image in half to print it onto two A4 pieces of cardstock.

After printing I taped them together. Meanwhile, I iron some good, stiff interfacing onto a large piece of the red fabric. Then I traced the image (mirrored, one facing left, the other facing right) onto the reinforced pieces. I pinned the interfaced fabric lions to the hip gore pieces. Reinforcing the fabric made it so much easier to maintain the shape as I was pinning and stitching.

The longest step was using a wide, tight (nearly buttonhole) stitch to slowly outline the every curve and claw of those two lions. I carefully cut them out and pinned them onto the hip gores of the dress. The last step was stitching them onto the fabric. I found that a medium to long zigzag stitch worked well, going over the edging in the same thread color I used to outline the lions.

The final product (above), stitched onto the hip gores. The lengthening I did is evident, but it achieved the right proportions for the applique.

Bonus Cersei Stuff!

The Belt- The key for this belt is having some decorative metal elements. My husband was the mastermind behind this- starting with four pieces of machined aluminum, he added holes for the metal rings and other decorative elements. He shaped the four pieces to fit a curved surface (my waist) and I assisted with a dry brush technique for antiquing the surface color. I then attached large gold chains from the sides to a single clasp at the back, like a necklace closure, but on a larger scale.

Hair & Makeup- Cersei has long, wavy, dark golden blonde hair, but affordable wig options tend to be white blonde(Khaleesi), light blonde, or brown, so I chose a light blonde style. I eventually made a crown from bakeable clay that hid the cheap wig hairline, and (even later) bought a metal crown/tiara. The makeup was an important part of capturing the Cersei look, the dark dramatic eyebrows in particular. Not used to enhancing my brows, I watched tutorial videos, and practiced.

You may also want to practice her sneer… if just for fun.

The Necklace- Using Sculpey, I also made a medallion pendant by pressing a large lion's head button into clay. Once it dried, I used that as a mold and pressed fresh bakeable clay into it to create the medallion.

Note: I used cling film in between the dried and fresh clay so it was easily removed. You need some sort of lining or release spray to keep it from sticking. Once the impression was made, I cleaned up the edges, made a hole for a necklace chain, and I was done! After baking the clay medallion in the oven I used metallic spray paint, and then gave it a layer of clear acrylic paint. Spray paint can remain "sticky" feeling on some materials, and a clear coat eliminates that while also protecting the finish.

Accessories- Besides that famous sneer, I searched high and low for a good "Cersei" goblet. I paired that with a glass carafe, I think it was from the 70's, with a scrolled metal handle and neck. My husband bought a Lannister banner and mounted it on a pole, carrying it with us for a fun backdrop.

Patches vs Appliqués vs Cutouts
What's in a Name?

Patches: Patches are pieces of fabric sewn or adhered onto a garment to cover a hole, or create a designs/embellishment.

Appliqués: Appliqués involve sewing or gluing a piece of fabric onto another to create designs or shapes.

Cutouts: Cutouts are intentional openings created in fabric, often forming shapes or patterns. This technique can add visual interest and playfulness to a design, allowing the underlying fabric or skin to peek through.

Gown with lace cutout back

Creating Appliqués: Material Considerations

- **A Delicate Flower:** Keep in mind that your entire garment will need the washing and care of the most delicate/picky material that you use. If one fabric going into it needs handwashing, that means the entire outfit will have to be washed by hand. Otherwise you risk that one fabric shrinking/fading/warping.

- **That's Heavy, Doc:** The weight of the fabric your garment is made from and the weight of the patches don't need to be the same, BUT consider the stress on the fabric that is getting the addition of the patch. If it is too delicate it may not hold up to the extra weight.

- **A Bit of a Stretch:** If your base material has stretch content, the applique could pull the fabric down or warp the shape. At the very least, a non-stretch applique on stretch fabric means that you'll lose the stretch in that area, which could impact the functionality of your costume

- **A Cut Above:** A great way to create drama is to create a large applique with openings or mesh areas. Lay it onto your costume piece, pin it in place, and stitch it down. Then turn it over, and carefully remove the fabric from the open/mesh areas with a scissors. (As pictured)

Attachment Methods

Sewing: For durability, sew patches and appliqués on with a zigzag stitch around the edges. If the patch is very large you may want some stitching on the interior as well. The thread should be the same color or slightly darker, as colors lighter than the patch will stand out.

Fabric Glue: You can use fabric glue or fusible webbing, but keep in mind that they may not hold up to washings as well as stitched patches. Plus, the glue or webbing may show behind thin or lacy appliques. Apply a thin layer of fabric glue, press down firmly, and let it dry fully.

Fusible Webbing: If using fusible webbing, cut a piece the size and shape of your applique and place it on the back of your patch. Place your patch/applique on the costume piece. Use just a couple pins to keep it in place, because you'll be ironing it on from the inside of your fabric. Be sure your fabric can stand up to the heat needed to adhere the webbing, or use a protective ironing cloth. Let the iron sit on the patch for a couple seconds just to keep it in place, then remove the pins. Turn the item back over and set the webbing with the hot iron for the recommended amount of time in the instructions.

Iron-On Options: Some patches and appliqués come with adhesive backing. Place them on the garment, cover with a pressing cloth, and apply heat with an iron. If they are very thick or beaded, follow the fusible webbing suggestions above. You may want to augment the permanence of adhesive backed appliques with stitching, but keep in mind that the glue will gum up your needles.

Unusual Methods: You could also experiment with different methods of attaching your appliques. Rivets would create a more armor-like or industrial look, while lacing a satin ribbon along the edge could give a more fairytale effect. Get creative! Just be sure to make sure the attachment is secure, and that you have done what you need to be sure the edges of your applique won't fray.

Design Time

- *What's the Big Idea:* Start by sketching your ideas or finding some inspiration or source images.

- *What Will They Think of Next?:* If you're replicating a logo or emblem for a cosplay you may be able to print it for the pinning stages below, or even use printable polyester sheets made for laser printers to make your patch exactly as you want it.

- *Paper Dolls:* Cut the design out of paper first, and lay iit onto the costume to help get the sizing and placement just right.

- *A Good Foundation:* Use a sturdy material for the base of your applique. The last thing you want is to get a couple layers in only to find out that your base is too flimsy to hold up to the weight of your design/embellishments.

- *Propa Placement:* Consider body movement and how it will interact with other elements of the costume. Will it catch on an armguard? Does it rub against another part of the costume when you sit? Pinning the paper version on can be a way of bringing problems to your attention.

Chapter Five

Faux Scalemail
Two Unique Approaches

Scalemail

Making scalemail/scalemaille is a skill.
It is expensive to buy because it's a learned skill, and worth the money.

If I could afford to commission scalemaile every time I needed some, I would. But, alas, I do not have the money for all the things I would like, and so I have embraced creative alternatives that lend me some flexibility in achieving a scalemail look.
I will always encourage you to patronize local makers. Or to learn this skill yourself! And then make me something beautiful because I inspired you so.

This chapter goes over two techniques to get a scalemail look if you do not have the skill or funds to make or buy actual scalemail, or if one of these alternatives work better for your specific costume needs.

The first type is a leather scalemail that I made for a Jaime Lannister costume. Naturally, you can use faux leather or another material that these techniques would work on.

The second type uses purchased metal scales, but involves sewing them onto a fabric base instead of linking them with metal rings. (Crocheted scalemail is also a product I've seen, and seems like a creative option as well!)

A Leather Take

Though the costumer designers for Game of Thrones pulled inspiration from various corners of the planet as well as various historical periods, there is intentional consistency, particularly within family groups or by character region (such as fitted shoulders on Lannister jackets and hip gores on their robes, the studded details of the Ironborn, the plentiful fur trims of the northern families).

What this means when cosplaying the show's characters is that there is some flexibility in construction and design choices, even if you're the type to usually go with historically accurate details or techniques (as discussed

in Chapter 3). The goal is to achieve the look, and it's easier to take a little creative license in achieving that when the character is not set in a specific time period. I chose the most iconic Jaime Lannister look; the Captain of the Kingsguard armor. However the prospect of buying yards of beautiful, oiled, *accurate* leather for a long coat was rather cost prohibitive.

Instead, I found a great silk blend woven drapery fabric in a $6 bag at a thrift store and had enough for the coat *and* the hip gores on Cersei's costume as well. That made me a happy camper! I used McCall's pattern 4745 for this jacket because I had 9 days to complete both Jaime and Cersei. The double breasted style and length were also appropriate for my goals. A thrift-ed sand-colored curtain would make an excellent cape, and I was repainting a version of a Roman soldier chestplate for the armor (see chapter 13). Believe it or not, repainted plastic knight armor from the Dollar Store worked as the pauldrons and the base of the lower half. But the golden scalemail was a distinctive aspect that I needed to get creative to figure out- after all, I certainly didn't know how to make chainmail!

Leather Scalemail

I had some thin leather that I had planned to use for a book making project a good number of years ago. I took that leather and spray painted the unfinished side dark gold. On the finished side I marked lines to cut out a massive amount of 1 x 2 inch diamonds, and let my rotary mat and blade do the rest.

More of the jacket material served as base for the scales. I cut out my desired size and shape for the armor panels, and finished the edges in the sewing machine. Using the longest stitch, I started at the bottom of the panel. I sewed across the top section of each diamond, placing them so the center of each diamond overlapped the next slightly as I went. The next line began about an inch up to ensure overlap.

The end result, though it could have been more orderly (and I would certainly measure everything more precisely if I were doing it again now), looks like golden scalemail for zero cost, since I happened to have the leather and spray paint.

29

Final Result? A respectable and recognizable Jaime, though not completely faithful to the show costume.

Handsewn Scalemail

This was not for a costume, but rather a dress I was modifying to wear during post-con hours at Tesla-Con. I wanted to do something unique but not too complex, as I spend all day at Teslacon in corset, bustle, and full Victorian gear more often than not.

I happened to have a couple bags of aluminum scales I had bought some years before, when I imagined I would be augmenting a couple pieces of armor. I had used a few scales in outfits here and there, but the bulk sat untouched. I had two sizes, in both black and silver.

I bought a blue dress with one sleeve and an asymmetrical neckline.

This took SO long. Truly.

The Plan was to have the scales down one side and from the shoulder down the arm. What ended up being made was scales down one side. I greatly underestimated how many I needed vs how many I had, and so plans changed, as it was one week until the convention!

The fabric of the dress was very stretchy so I knew I would want a sturdier base. I ripped out the side seam and inserted a 4" panel of metallic silver fabric I had in my fabric stash. I laid out a few sample rows, but it was

difficult to keep the scales in place, as they slid around when overlapping. So I laid them next to each other in the patterns I wanted, but this didn't give an accurate representation of how many I needed.

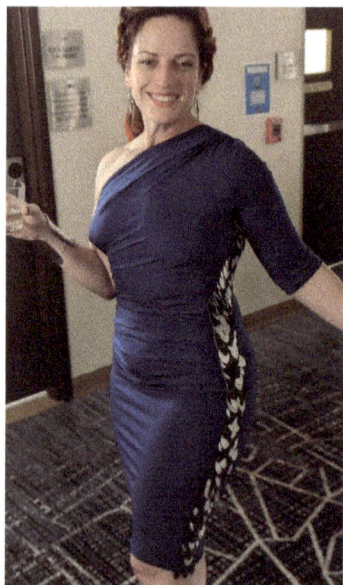

The final result!

Additionally, they needed to be overlapped by the next row by 50% of their length. It was literally one inch of progress at a time.

Before I was done with the first row I went back and switched out to a heavier thread. Before I was done with the second row, I was doing a stitch at the top of each scale's hole, then one from the center to the right, and from the center to the left. They just moved around too much otherwise. For both maille techniques- start at the base and work your way up

I'm going to be honest, I don't think this took less time than if someone skilled in the craft had made a panel of scalemail. If I had more than a week before the event I'd probably have just ordered it from my favorite chainmailler, Rogue Maille.

Leather Scalemail Tips

- *Measure Twice, Cut Once:* Once you've decided on the size/shape, make a template to ensure uniformity. Take your time when cutting to minimize irregularities.

- *Go Long!:* Use long stitches, and backstitch or tie ends off (Hand sewing is also an option if you don't have a machine, but see tip #1 below.)

- *Some Extra Oomph:* Use a background fabric that will make your scales pop. A dark fabric will keep the focus on the scales. A metallic that hints at the color of the scales could make any tiny gaps virtually disappear.

- *Bring it on Down:* Don't stitch too high on the scale- this can make them unstable, likely to flop in multiple directions, and it's easier for the leather (depending on thickness) to tear. Stitch ⅓ of the way down the scale.

Handsewn Scalemail Tips

- *Give Atropos No Quarter:* Make sure you're using heavy enough thread. After all, it will have to hold up to metal rubbing against it. I would suggest an upholstery weight thread.

- *Weight, What?:* Even aluminium scales are heavy, so keep the durability of your fabric in mind, and be aware that if it has stretch content the scales could drag it down or warp the shape. Additionally, too much stretch can pull or break the threads keeping your scales on!

- *Spacing Out:* Assume you will lose about half the width and half the height for overlap, though this varies by size, because the hole in each scale is larger, proportionately, the smaller the scale is. So it takes up a larger percentage of the scale and must be covered.

- *All in a Row:* You'll want to test the stability of the scale positioning- will your scales stay in place or go off to one side? This could mean more stabilizing stitches are needed, but it could just be a result of the angle the scales are at, or the way the costume piece moves. Testing it after a row or two may save you a headache later on!

- *Stick to It:* Plan out your pattern in advance using putty or something similar to keep the scales in place with the necessary overlap. The overlap causes you to use more scales than you'd think!

But I was in the situation I was in, and so I continued to stitch the scales on, alternating the colors and sizes. Once I got into the rhythm, and accepted the inevitable shortage of scales for my original goal, I made good progress.

I finished the dress over three nights, and when I walk in it I make a swishing sound, like money.

Well, like loose change.

Chapter 5 Cover Model: Richard Kern
Jaime Lannister Photographer: Kate Peterson

Chapter Six

A Pirate's Life For Me
French Seams, ShirtPlackets, Pirate" Cuffs

The Dread Pirate Roberts

The Dread Pirate Roberts was a labor-of-love costume that went through a few iterations. The first version was made with an accompanying Buttercup dress… yes, the quintessential couple's costume.

On first glance, the monochromatic marauder's costume seems very simple. Black pants and black leather boots with turned over cuffs. A black shirt that partially laces up the front and a black head scarf. Plus black leather accessories in the form of a mask, gloves and belt for the rapier scabbard. He also wears a wide black cloth belt, tied at the hip.

But upon closer inspection, this classic shirt is timeless; the flowing silhouette and deep cuffs reflect the adventurous spirit of the high seas. It's a staple for any aspiring swashbuckler or historical reenactor. The costume was made quickly, for an event, so after a few years I decided to give the shirt an upgrade. Bear in mind that due to the fullness of the sleeves, you'll want to choose a densely woven but still somewhat light-weight fabric for the shirt.

Ironically, I made a shirt for the distinctly NOT piratey Ichabod Crane costume, as discussed in Chapter 7, using most of these techniques. The cuffs aren't as deep and they button, and the shirt doesn't lace up the front placket, but these finishing techniques are useful beyond outfitting seabound vagabonds (as modeled by Ichabod on the next page).

This chapter, set up just a little differently than the others, will guide you through the making of these traditional pirate shirt features; a traditional placket, deep cuffs, and French seams. You can draft or buy a pattern, being sure that a turned over collar, full sleeves, and a closed or lacing front with extra room in the shirt body are all included features.

This chapter IS a bit heavier on sewing than most of the others, so if you are not a sewist, feel free to enjoy the pictures and perhaps bookmark the chapter for a future challenge!

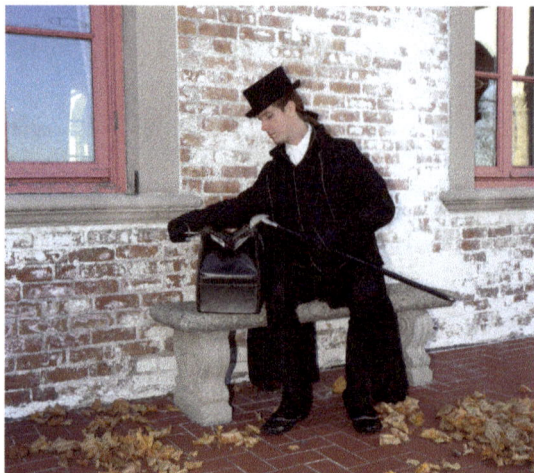

He's hiding a whole floofy shirt under there!

French Seams

Note- French seams are a finishing technique. They are a fantastic way to finish the edges of a garment, providing a clean, professional look while preventing fraying.

Anyone who sews quickly learns that you sew fabric with the "right sides together". However, for French seams, it's just the opposite.

To start, you'll want to begin with the wrong sides of the fabric facing each other. Align the edges carefully and sew a narrow seam, typically about 1/4 inch wide. This is narrower than seams are usually sewn, but this initial seam is key; it should be precise since it sets the foundation for the rest of the process.
PINNING is your friend here.

Once you've sewn the first seam, trim that tiny seam allowance by about half, down to about a mere 1/8 inch to reduce bulk. This can be nerve wracking.

Then, turn the fabric right sides together, enclosing the raw edges. Again, pin! Pinning is your friend!

Press the seam to ensure everything lays flat, and sew another seam, this time about 3/8 inch from the edge. This second seam will encase the raw edges of the first seam, creating a neat finish. Go slowly the first couple times, to ensure you catch all of the raw edge within this encasement.

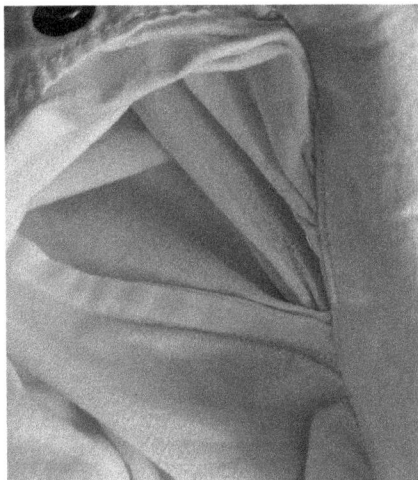

Interior shoulder seam, so clean!

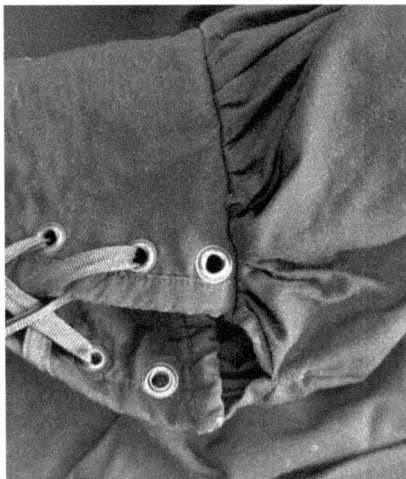

Cuff seam, bulkier with gathers but still clean.

Finally, give it a good press, and you'll have beautifully finished seams that not only look great but also add durability to your project. French seams are especially ideal for lightweight and delicate fabrics, as they enhance the garment's overall appearance while maintaining a soft feel.

The concept of the French seam is essential in my technique to achieving perfect sheer hems, as discussed in chapter 15.

Making a Placket

The placket is the reinforced center front opening of the shirt, which could extend from several inches to all the way down the front, as with button-front shirts. The shorter openings allow the shirt to be put on over the head easily, and the placket ensures that it is stable enough for lacing, buttons, etc. Some plackets are made to lay flat without any method for maintaining closure, like those seen on some kaftan robe styles.

Mark the opening: Mark the line down the center of the shirt from where the placket should start, at the opening of the collar, to where you want it to end, probably several inches down. Use tailor's chalk, a temporary marking pen, or even pins…. This is not a permanent line.

Cut the Placket: When you cut the rectangle of fabric for the placket, ensure that you give it a few inches beyond your planned opening on each side, and the bottom, plus seam allowance.

- *DO use interfacing! It will really affect the final look, trust me.*

- Cut a piece of interfacing the same size as the placket and fuse or baste it to the wrong side of the fabric.

Sew the Placket to the Shirt: Wrong sides together (it's a theme in this chapter), center the placket on the shirt front.

- Pin it in place, making a line all the way down your planned opening, but *don't* cut it yet.

- Using your marking and line of pins as a guide, sew a line of stitching ⅝" around it, making 3 sides of a rectangle.

- NOW cut down the center of the stitched fabrics. At the bottom, clip at an angle to the ⅝" seam corners.

- Then turn the fabrics right side out, press (this will really help!), and stitch together. That's it!
Now you can add your grommets, buttonholes, or whatever closure you like!

Good, bad.... I'm the guy with the cleavage.

Creating Deep Cuffs

Note- The cuff length plus your sleeve length should NOT equal your regular sleeve length. It should be longer by several inches, so that the sleeve above the cuff has that full, billowing, romantic, dramatic, etc. piratey look.

- **Prepare the Cuffs:**

Cut two rectangles for each cuff, the width you want plus seam allowance. If you choose to cut the rectangles a little wider at the top of the cuff, don't overdo the angle… an extra inch goes a long way. You can always cut them a little bigger and lay them along your forearms to test the size.

Attach interfacing to the inside if desired for structure. This could be stitchable or iron-on, but if using iron-on make sure the side that has the interfacing ends up being on the inside of the cuff. The reason for that is because, after several washes, if the

I used interfacing for the deep cuffs

iron-on interfacing reacts even slightly differently than your fabric, it can result in a strange bubbled look on the interfaced fabric surface. Better to have it on the inside where it will still do its job, unseen.

- **Sew the Cuffs:**

Sew along the bottom and side edges and turn the cuff right side out.

- **Attach to Sleeves:**

Gather the sleeve edge slightly and pin the cuff to the sleeve. If your sleeve is very full you may want to pre-gather it to the length you need to fit it on the cuff top, and stitch the gathers down.

Sew in place, using the French seam technique to finish. Remember, this will be with wrong sides together first, with a very narrow seam, then trim, turn it to right sides together, and encase those raw edges in another seam. Press...

And enjoy your beautiful shirt, you dastardly scallywag!

Chapter Six Cover Model: James Opalewski
Chapter Six Cover Photographer: Kate Peterson
Ichabod Crane Model: Richard Kern
Ichabod Ctane Photographer: Robert Remme

Chapter Seven

Getting Detailed with Tailoring
Menswear/Tailoring Details

"You don't need to conjure up new treasures when you can bring old gems into the light." Or, to put it another way, you don't need to reinvent the wheel.

With Halloween around the corner and a few upcoming conventions in my calendar, it was time for me to take on two Victorian menswear, yet still very different, challenges: Ichabod Crane from Tim Burton's Sleepy Hollow, and a steampunk men's coat straight from the instructions of an authentic Victorian pattern.

Neither project would be a quick throw-together, but with enough determination (and coffee), I knew I could make both feel truly "mine." Or, rather, my husband's.

This chapter will take you through the process of the creation of these two costumes with a focus on some classic tailoring details often found in menswear (though certainly not exclusively).

Let's start with Ichabod.

Ichabod Crane

I'm a sucker for Burton's whimsical dark aesthetic, and Johnny Depp's Ichabod Crane, with his devil-may-care waves of hair falling across his oversized eyes, and his scientific albeit terrified nature, has always stood out to me. It's a look that's seemingly simple but takes a few key pieces to make it instantly recognizable.

I wanted to channel Ichabod's iconic quirkiness and tortured Victorian charm, while acknowledging the challenge that making my first menswear coat would present. It would be worth it, as I was making a Katrina van Tassel costume to go with it... couple's costumes ftw! (See details on that dress in chapter 3!)

The Research:

Before I even picked up a needle, I went on a deep dive.
This wasn't just about getting a few measurements right—this was about

capturing the essence of Ichabod. I rewatched Sleepy Hollow, taking note of his coat's high collar, the collar echoed in his vest, his deeply cuffed jacket, and the cravat at the peak of the flowing shirt he wears throughout his misadventures. It wasn't about perfect replication; it was about interpreting the look for myself, while keeping true to the character's eccentricities.

The entire outfit was heavy on dark tones—grays, blacks, browns—yet very elegant. His coat, especially, had distinctive piping around the cuffs, the collar, and down the front. The vest had similar piping.
I also noted the accessories: his cravat, his unusual glasses, and of course the medical bag full of instruments of his own design. The trick was to find fabrics and patterns that evoked his look but didn't require me to hunt down a perfectly identical jacket from 1799.

Woo! (Ichabod wooing Katrina)

The Materials:

The most important part of this look was the coat. I knew I'd have to make it from scratch, but where to start? After much deliberation, I chose fabric sturdy enough to give structure but with just a touch of stretch, for comfort. The coat and vest would use the same fabric.

The shirt was fairly simple—the time period called for a billowing, piratey white cotton affair (similar to the Dread Pirate Roberts shirt I made in chapter 6), with oversized sleeves to capture Ichabod's unkempt, "I've been running away from an evil specter all day" vibe. The cravat, a long, wide length of fabric, was made from the same cotton.

The Making:

First, I tackled the coat. Ichabod's coat has that high dramatic collar, so I designed mine with a reinforced collar that could stand stiff on its own. The coat's fit was a challenge. I knew it had to be slim-fitting but not restrictive, with a flare at the bottom to give it that slight gothic drama. I added strategic darts in the back on either side of the vent to accentuate the waist but kept the silhouette from being too tight.

The vest, once finished, fit like a glove, but I made it a little longer than in the film to create a more elongated, silhouette-stretching effect, especially because the person I was making it for was over six feet tall.

The highlight of both the vest and coat, for me, was the piping detail. The fabric end of the costume was finished off with a pair of boots from his closet, worn enough to pass off as having been stomping through the mud all day in pursuit of the Horseman.

The final touch? An antique doctor's bag I bought on Ebay, along with a turn of the century medical book. We had fun filling that bag with glass jars full of herbs, vintage medical tools, and even a handmade replica of the optical illusion Ichabod presented to Katrina in the film- a circular paper with an empty cage on one side, a cardinal on the other. When twisted by attached strings, it appears that the cardinal is caged. I was very proud of myself.

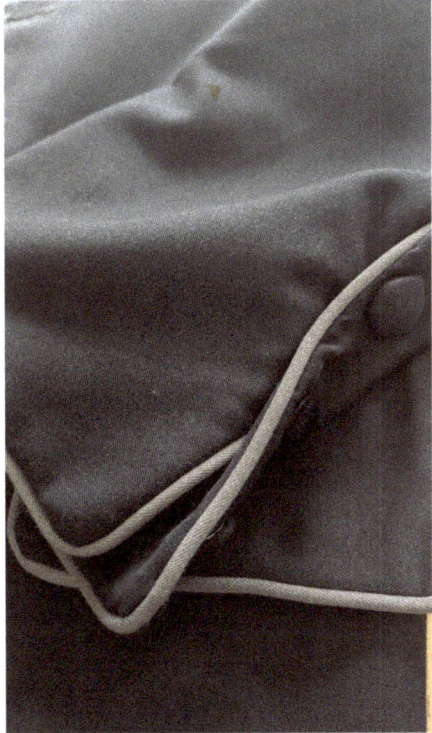

What Did I Learn?

Looking back on this very-long-ago project, I wish I had found a fabric with more structure, or used more reinforcement, either in the use of canvas in key areas at the shoulders and cuff, or with regular interfacing.

The edge piping is a nice finish!

I feel that, although the less structured look fits with Ichabod's character, sharper shoulders, etc. would have been more true to the movie costume.

The Steampunk Frock Coat

Alright, onto the brass tacks! After diving into the darkness of Sleepy Hollow, it was time for something even more… eccentric?

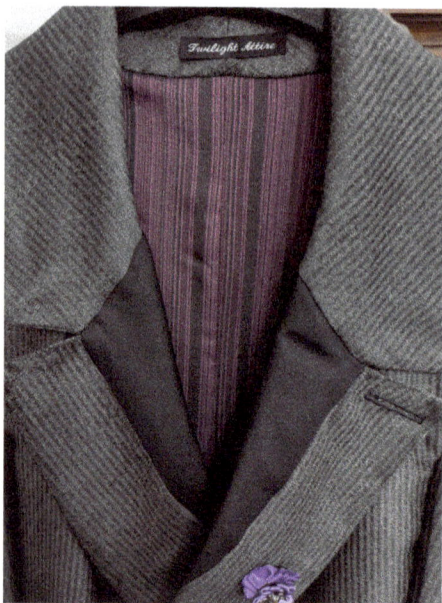

A nice clean finish.

Enter the steampunk frock coat. A bit of history, a lot of imagination, and plenty of drama. My self-imposed challenge with this one? I owned a book of authentic patterns (pictured below) which you could transfer onto paper in true proportions, then resize to your own measurements. Frock coats were actually trending down by the late Victorian period/turn of the century, in favor of the modern sack coat.

The Materials:
For this project, I found a deep blue/dark grey fabric that had a thin, almost monochromatic stripe. The fabric had the density and sheen of waxed denim, but also a touch of stretch on the content. It would serve as the body of the coat because I wanted something that felt formal and clean without screaming "antique". The lining was a medium weight purple and black striped polyester for a fun and distinctive pop of color.

The Making:
The process of transferring the pattern from book to paper is thus: make sure your paper is very large. In your book, the pattern image will show that the shoulder line is 6" long, with the outside edge 1" lower than the inner edge, and so you mark a 6" long line on your paper that dips an inch on one side. The pattern book shows that the center back line is 18" long, from the inside shoulder edge. So you mark a line down 18". And so on for 24 measurements.

At *that* point, you have the actual pattern, but in the size they specify, usually by chest and waist measurements. So at that point you begin altering the pattern to the measurements of the person who will actually be wearing it. This is done by applying percentage changes to the pieces according to the difference between the original and the desired sizes. I know this because I do it with original corset pattern measurements all the time, when the difference between lines on the pattern could be ⅛" because you're dividing a 1.5" difference between 12 seams on 6 pattern pieces.

SO. That was actually the most mind-numbing part of the process. But given the appeal of making an *authentic* Victorian pattern…. nope, it was still mind-numbing.

The rest of it was mostly just sewing the pieces together. I put an interior pocket into the lining, and made a matching vest with welt pocket from the lining material while I was at it. Welt pockets are the little pockets on the front of vests that seem to have one neat little line indicating an opening. Welt pockets intimidated me for a while. Not as long as buttonholes did, but for a bit. I pored over the instructions written in the patterns, still scratching my head at how these darn things were supposed to go together. I just couldn't see it in my head.

Finally, I looked up a couple of videos, and actually seeing the process made it click what the instructions were trying to say. Everyone learns differently, but this one was a challenge for me. When you take on welt pockets, don't be afraid to check out a play-by-play online!
The lining was sewn, right sides together, up the center front, along the collar and down the other center front, and then I hand stitched it at the inside of the armholes.

What Did I Learn?
Honestly, though the coat fabric had a decent amount of structure, I could have used some reinforcement at the shoulders and collar. I feel that this *is* one area that I'm still lacking in experience, primarily because I am not often making coats and structured outerwear. I have determined that the next coat project will be more structured.

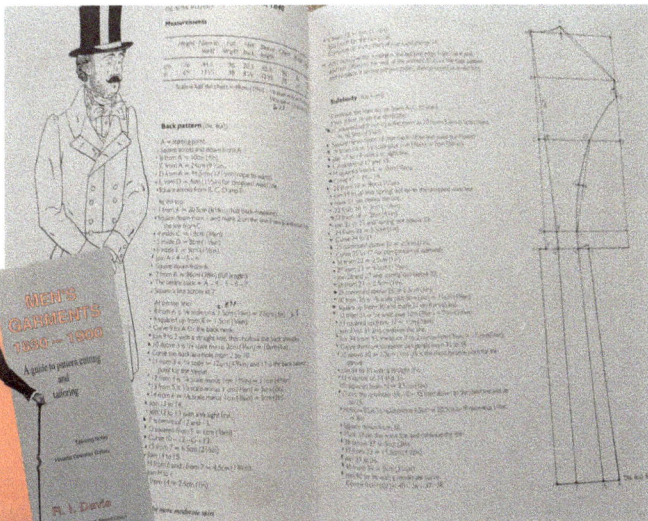

Just the first page of measurements I needed.

The Results?

Visually, Ichabod Crane's costume turned out to be exactly what I hoped for—quirky, distressed, and perfectly in line with Tim Burton's twisted take on the character. My husband felt every bit the nervous, inquisitive detective on a ghostly hunt, and the piping provided a subtle but sophisticated elevation to both the coat and vest. As for the steampunk coat? Let's just say you could step onto a dirigible and blend right in, in the best way. The waxed denim look of the fabric along with the subtle stripe was the perfect way to give a Victorian frock coat an alternate-history feel.

In the end, both of these costumes taught me the same thing: it's not about recreating every last detail. It's about making the costume your own—putting your own personality and your creativity into the work. Also, reinforce your jackets.

Welt Pockets

- **Choosing the Right Fabric:** Select a non-stretch fabric that holds structure well, such as wool or a blend. Lighter or stretch fabrics could sag over time.

- **Pattern Preparation:** Trust me, watch a video. I went cross-eyed looking at the instruction pictures, trying to make sense of them. Once I watched a video of how the welt was laid out, it all made sense.

- **Sewing the Welts:** Make the pocket bag just a bit bigger than you think you'll need it, at least the first time. There's nothing more frustrating than setting a perfect welt pocket only to find that the seam allowances ate up more of your space than you expected.

- **Finishing Touches:** Reinforce the edges of the pocket with a zigzag stitch or serger to prevent fraying. This reduces the chance of developing a hole in the bottom of your pocket.

A lining that pops can add a lot!

Adding Edge Piping

- *Selecting Piping Fabric:* If your fabric has no stretch, consider cutting strips for the piping on the bias (at a 45 degree angle to the weave of the fabric). This helps the piping bend around curves (like collars and cuffs).

- *Incorporating Piping:* Use a zipper foot when possible to allow for precise sewing close to the cording without disturbing the main fabric. You'll get a closer stitching line & do less fighting with layers of **fabric.**

- *Sewing Technique:* Slow down! Take your time, really, because you really don't want to do this twice. Pin or clip your layers together as often as you need to, pins perpendicular to the sewing line.

The final vest buttons, buttonholes, and THE welt pocket (well, one of them).

Reinforcing Interiors

- *Choosing Reinforcement Materials:* Depending on the level of support needed. Choose a lightweight interfacing for areas requiring flexibility, and a heavier canvas for more structured areas like the collar and shoulders.

- *Application:* Cut interfacing to the same size as the coat pieces. Interfacing is sewn onto the interior of the lining, between the outer fabric and the lining. Historically, and even now in formal jackets, pieces of cotton canvas were often used at the shoulders and collar to help hold the shape of the area, attached to the seam allowances of the interior when not sewn alongside the lining, to keep the stitches from showing.

- *Sewing Techniques:* When attaching reinforcements, use a basting stitch for a secure hold. A row of zigzag stitching around the edges of the interfacing can prevent it from shifting during wear.

By learning the techniques of welt pockets, edge piping, and interior reinforcements, you'll enhance the functionality of your garments and the sophistication of the final look. With practice and attention to detail, you'll be able to produce costumes that stand the test of time, even becoming wardrobe staples for any occasion.

Chapter 7 Cover Model: James Opalewski
Photographer: Robert Remme

Photographer: Laura Meyer

Chapter Eight

No Paint, No Gain
Fabric Pens & Hand Painting Fabric

"The more that you read, the more things you will know. The more that you learn, the more places you'll go."- Dr. Seuss

Come with me, as I lead you, in this chapter, through the previously unknown jungles of fabric painting. I have journeyed into these lands out of necessity, as so many of us do on our costuming adventures.

Three costumes, in particular, have required the learning of these new skills; Xevv Bellringer from the show "The Lexx", Mrs. Lovett from "Sweeney Todd: Demon Barber of Fleet Street", and the character of Siren Maya from the game "Borderlands 3".

Maya is the most recent costume, and the most involved as far as fabric painting, so I'll dig into the most detail with that process.

Xevv Bellringer

First! If you have not seen this tongue-in-cheek, over the top sci-fi show dripping with innuendo and cheese-ball humor…. run, don't walk, to find it, if you can. The show ran from 1997-2002, so this quirky and highly original Canada-based series may have escaped your notice.

I created the costume for Xevv Bellinger, the defiant woman who escaped her fate as a love slave when a freak accident during the dumbing-down device fused her DNA with that of a cluster lizard (think The Fly, but more fierce).

I also made the costumes of her shipmates; Kai, her undead assassin crush, 790, the unbodied robot head desperately in love with her, and Stanley Tweedle, the security guard turned ship captain that *no-one* has a crush on.

For the purposes of this chapter, though, we'll focus on Xevv. Her outfit consists of a cropped top, short skirt, and big knee-high boots. The story goes, she made her clothing from cluster lizard hide and pieces of industrial rubber to hold the pieces of hide together.
(I know, I know, but *I* didn't write the story).

So there is a lizard-like pattern on the segmented sections of the tops, as well as on the front and back of the skirt.

The fabric I found for the costume was a tan sueded upholstery fabric, and it has held up (obviously) over 20 years, so I have no complaints. I draped the costume pieces, placing and measuring from my dressform instead of trying to find or alter patterns for the top and skirt.

After making and sewing the costume together, I used fabric paints and stiff bristled brushes in a couple different sizes to create the pattern, referencing images from the show.

The texture of the suede held paint well, and gave an extra impression of depth.

In addition to the pattern, I also did some shading to add depth in the corners and at edges.
Even after 20 years, this outfit is a match for any cluster lizard lurking around the corner.

Mrs. Lovett

The next fabric painting challenge was Mrs. Lovett.
I'm a big fan of Tim Burton flicks in general, and it's hard for me to resist a nice dark idea for a couple's costume, so when "Sweeney Todd" came out, making the Mrs. Lovett costume was just about a given. As discussed in chapter 3, the biggest question mark was around which of her costumes from the film to create, and I landed on the early,

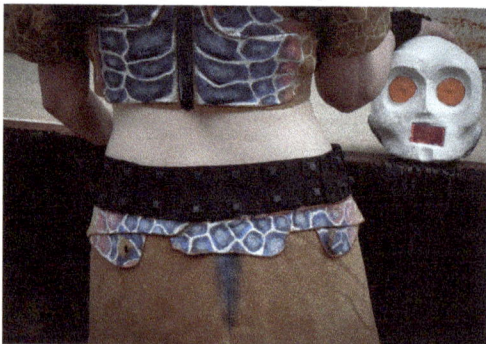

49

flour-coated skirt, & corset top she has on in her bakehouse when she "meets" Sweeney Todd. (But we all know that she knew him years before, when he was innocent young Benjamin.) Some quality promotional costume shots of Helena Bonham Carter provided me with more detail than the intentionally dismal lighting of the film alone. Frazzled trims and hints of ragged red fabric around the edges of her off-the-shoulder top hinted at her infernal activities, and the bare shoulders are almost bawdy for the times!

Her skirt, ruffled down the back, was in a muddled brown/grey fabric with an oversized paisley pattern. Red bloomers edged with black lace and black and red striped hose hid beneath the skirt. The plain black corset was the easiest part for me- I already had made one about a year before that would work.

However, try as I might- and I did try- I couldn't find any fabric that even approached a similarity to the skirt. Resigned, I decided to hand paint the paisley pattern onto the fabric.

After making the skirt, I armed myself with a few black fabric pens from the local craft store. I examined the film images, and compared the design to other examples of paisleys I found online, to get familiar with the hallmarks of the pattern.

The process of painting the pattern on was not so difficult as it was lengthy. It took a loooong time. Fortunately, the skirt fabric was a plain cotton, had been prewashed, and had no stretch. That made the application pretty simple.

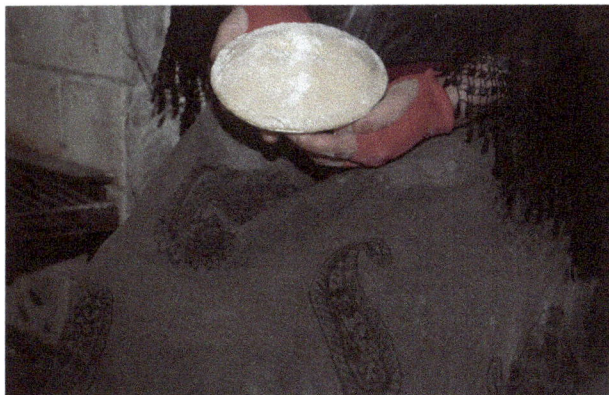

I had a thin square of wood that I clipped the fabric onto so I could work in manageable areas and not worry about the paint bleeding through onto anything on the other side. It turned out well, but I definitely think this is one of those things that wouldn't have been worth it if I weren't such a whiny baby about getting details just right.

Siren Maya

I usually don't need an excuse to make a costume, but that's how this one started. A fellow costumer friend had posted about getting a group together to a group costume shoot at an upcoming convention. The theme would be Borderlands 3. I hadn't seen the newly released film, but I'd played Borderlands 2 and 3 a number of years before, so I did a quick refresher on the characters online, and then I offered to contribute to the shoot as Siren Maya. That was welcomed, & I started to plan.

I thought "this will be a pretty quick and easy costume, and I have two months. No problem!" I would thrift a pair of pants and belt, perhaps shoes too. I'd see if I could find a black bodysuit online that would get me close, and the coat… the coat would be the coup de grace. In my basement, sitting for too many years, I had a black wool Edwardian coat. Long, fitted, with notched collar and flared hem. With a couple modifications, it would be perfect!

Some of the things in that plan came to pass. I found a bodysuit online and removed one long sleeve. I thrifted a belt to modify and used boots that I already owned. I removed both long sleeves from the black Edwardian coat. I planned to use yellow fabric spray paint on the lining of the coat and on the inside of the black hood I had cut and sewn, to mirror Maya's yellow lining.

That did NOT work out.
On the black interior of the coat I would have had to use easily $80 of spray paint to build enough yellow pigment to show, and at that point it would likely be stiff and scratchy. And as I tried to get enough paint to show on the inside of the (unlined) hood, it soaked through

51

and began showing on the outside. I went to plan B: I removed the coat lining, bought yellow cotton, and made a new lining for the coat and a hood version 2.0.

I learned from this lesson, though, going forward with the coat, and as I prepared to paint large sections, I taped them off and gave them a base coat of white as a sealing coat before doing anything else. Then I went back and cleaned up the edges where necessary with black paint.

I had to learn not to be timid in using white and black paint to create the contrast necessary for the cell-shading style. I kept taking a step back and realizing it wasn't enough.

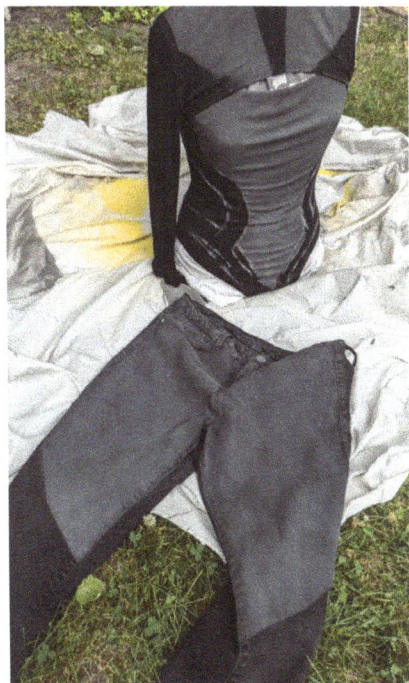

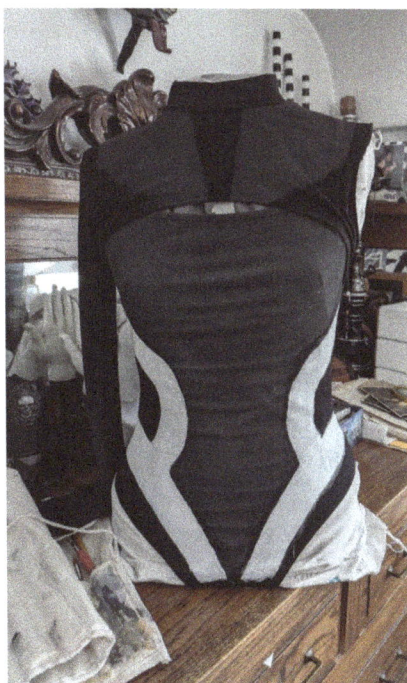

To create some of the textures on the surface of her coat, I cut apart a metal mesh pen cup, and dipped the curved surface into the paint. Tapping off extra paint first, I then pressed it onto the coat at different angles to get the look I wanted.
It was a lot of going back and forth between the paint job and reference photos.

For the white belt I found at a resale store, I attached a new buckle and used black marker for the cell shading. The ombre wig was very long and I had fun chopping it up (more on that in chapter 10).

But you're not going to believe this...

The morning of the convention I spent over an hour copying an ornate organic design onto my left arm with light blue body paint… I hadn't thought of the fact ahead of time that I am not right-handed. So that was cramp inducing. I'm going to try to paint the pattern onto a nylon sleeve, eliminating the need to paint it onto my arm every time I wear the costume. Didn't think of that one in time! I used a black fine-tipped liquid eyeliner pen to apply the cell shading lines on my face. As this was the final step in doing the makeup, I was nervous… big black marks if I messed up!

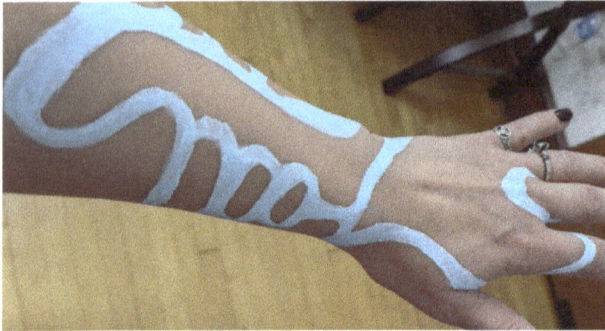

But generally I was very happy with how it turned out… It was good to explore fabric painting again after such a long hiatus!

Fabric Painting Essentials

- **Fabric:** Keep in mind that stretchy fabrics could cause your paint to crack over time. Thin fabrics will show the paint on the other side. The sueded fabric for Xevv's costume took paint well, and it didn't bleed through to the backing. It's always a good idea to test how your fabric will hold the paint.

- **Paint:** Be sure to use the right type of paint for your surface- fabric. Sometimes putting down a base layer of spray fabric paint is enough, and regular acrylic paint can easily be used on top of that.

- **Sealant:** A fabric medium or sealant is essential to protect the painted design and ensure durability. A spray sealant can be light and flexible.

- **Brushes and Tools:** You can use a variety of brushes—flat, round, and detail brushes—and sponges for blending. Tape and stencils can help achieve clean lines. Test the tape on the fabric you'll be using… some tapes aren't great at maintaining a seal at the edge, and others don't pull off easily. I used blue painter's tape, which was effective as long as I wasn't going overboard with paint at the edges.

Other Items: Get creative on ways to achieve different patterns on the fabric surface. I cut up a mesh pen holder to create a gridlike pattern on Maya's coat.

Getting Your Painting Techniques

- **Large Areas:** Start with the base colors. After taping off your areas to be painted, use a spray fabric paint or larger brush to apply a solid color to the main areas of the costume. For Maya, this was usually white or grey. Allow this layer to dry completely. Depending on the fabric paint's opacity, a second coat may be necessary for an even finish.

- **Fabric Colors:** Be aware that you'll need more layers of light colors to get them to show well on a dark background. A light coat of sealant as a base on your fabric can help mitigate this, and keep more of the paint from soaking into the fabric. Black fabric paint, when dry, will probably show up even if your fabric is black, due to the difference in blacks and any amount of sheen.

- **Details:** Once the base layer is dry, it's time to add more intricate details. For Maya's look, I used smaller brushes to create the unique cell shading that defines the animation style in the Borderlands series.

- **Pro-tip:** Start in the back. This was a new technique for me, so I started at the back of her bodysuit, which would usually be covered. That way, by the time I got to the front and the coat, I would have a better idea of how to achieve the look that I wanted. It's a learning process, so set yourself up for success!

Hand painting fabric can feel intimidating, but test out your techniques, take your time, and be kind to yourself. Hue got this!

Chapter 8 Cover Model: Roxanne Dobbs   Xevv Bellringer Model: Becky Benishek
Xevv Bellringer Photographer: Kate Peterson
Mrs. Lovett Photographer: Laura Meyer
Siren Maya Photographer: CosMeetupChicago

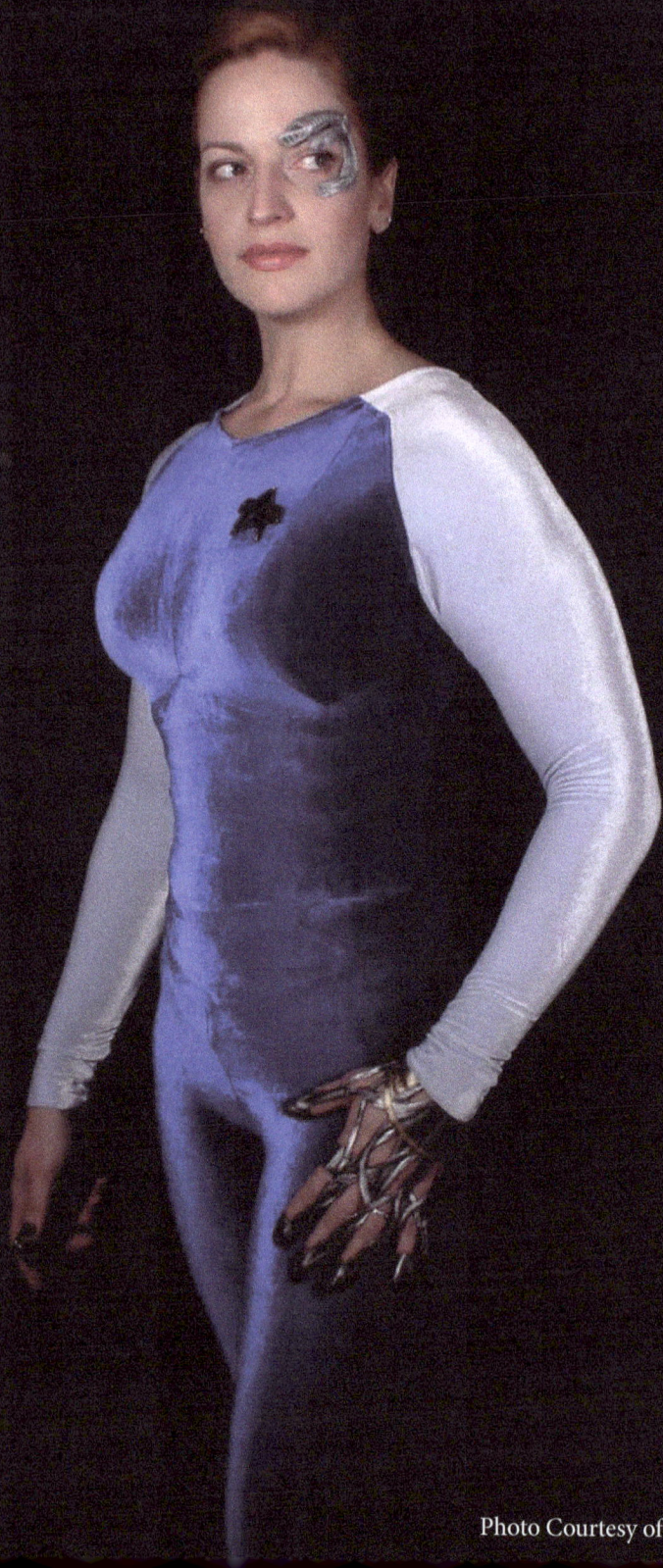

Chapter Nine

Laying It On Thick
Latex Prosthetics and Accessories

I was headed to a small convention in February one year, and I decided to keep it simple with only one costume per day; I pulled out a newer creation, the Evil Outfit of Evil (please see: the cover of this book!), and an old favorite that I hadn't worn in a couple of years, Seven of Nine from Star Trek: Voyager.

I am 100% biased in my belief that this character has one of the best character arcs in television, and her further character development in the Picard seasons (though not without its imperfections) have only served to reinforce that belief.

Anyways, cue to me pulling my outfits out of the basement and inspecting them for maintenance, mending needs, etc. "Evil" looked good (it usually does), but I had a rude lesson in how and where to store my accessories when it came to my Seven costume…. the facial prosthetics needed a repaint, and the nanoprobe exo-hand was badly deteriorated. The paint was cracked and flaking off in areas, and the rubber of the glove base had actually begun to disintegrate. Yikes.

With some paint I *could* have limped it through a day, maaaybe, but that is not how I costume.

I had one week to make a new glove. After some light research online into techniques others have used, I decided to make the second one in the same fashion as I had created the first.

The Glove
I began with a heavy rubber cleaning glove, believe it or not. I used a smaller size than last time- lessons learned- and used my original as a basis for planning. The glove had a band across the palm, caps over each finger and the thumb, and a closure (I used velcro) at the wrist. The lines on the back of the hand extended up the wrist, past where the sleeve of the bodysuit would cover.

The first step, though, was not cutting. This was another lesson learned; keeping the glove intact while I built the layers made for a more stable base as I worked. I used liquid latex to create the lines of the glove. With the first glove I planned to do layers of latex in order to build a three dimensional effect, but the liquid latex was so thin and took so long to dry adequately that I gave up after about six layers.

THIS time, however, I was using the *same* quart of liquid latex, from four(?) years earlier… and it had thickened considerably. So I planned out where my lines would go, and used a toothpick to scoop up the thick latex and lay it down in ropes along the back of the glove. I did three layers, and had beautiful results.

Of course, you may not want to wait for four years for your liquid latex to age, so you'll be happy to know that there are latex thickeners out there!

As you can see, the first layer created a good base, and the next two layers I worked to round off the top of the ropes, trying to make them look as much like nano-tubes (I suppose) as possible. Fortunately, because the latex was so old the drying time was likely shorter than it otherwise would have been for the amount I used.

Day three, and it was finally time to cut. An Exacto knife worked better than small scissors for precise cutting in all those interior spaces. A coat of black Plasti-dip spray served as the paint base for the glove. I dry-brushed metallic silver spray paint over the raised areas, letting the darker colored recessions do the hard work. For the wrist band closure, I hand stitched a square of velcro to each side.

If I had slowed down, I would have re-evaluated the design of my lines. They should have, in my new version, become more closely gathered and linear along the length of each finger and instead, I made them more random if anything. However, the depth and three-dimensionality resulting from the thicker latex and paint job gave a nicer overall look, and possibly a sturdier end product. The fit of the finger caps from the smaller size glove is more secure than in my original version, which makes for easier wear. Overall, I would say excellent results for a last minute project, though not perfect.

I will NOT be storing this prop in the basement, by the way.

My Latex Painting Tips

- **Preparation:** For better adhesion, clean the prosthetic with alcohol to remove any residue before painting.

- **Choosing Paints:** Flexible paint works best for latex.. Alcohol-based or silicone-based paints work well, as they won't crack when the latex moves. Acrylic paint can become rigid and may not adhere properly.

- **Base Layer:** Start with a dark base coat, or one that matches the skin tone of your character, if you're making a facial prosthetic. Apply the paint using a sponge or brush, that will allow for blending.

- **Detailing:** Once the base layer is dry, add details or texture using fine brushes or sponges.

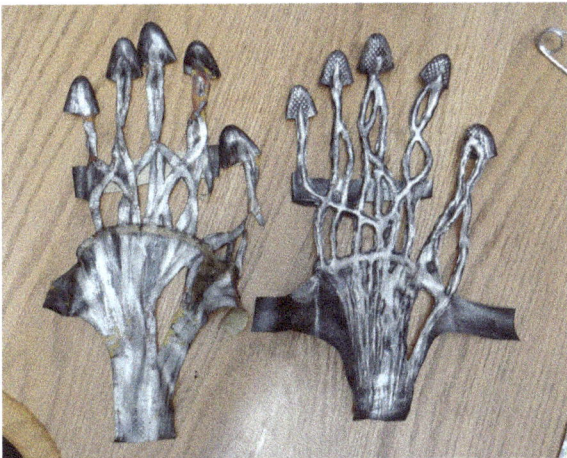

My Latex Adhering Tips

- **Preparing the Skin:** Always clean the area where the prosthetic will be applied with alcohol to remove oils and dirt. Esp if you may be sweating.

- **Choosing the Right Adhesive:** I had used spirit gum, and then eyelash glue, for years. I found the eyelash glue was less irritating, but neither held up well to movement or sweating. However, I got a great tip about Pros-Aide adhesive cream, and it's performed really well.

- **Application:** Apply a thin layer of adhesive to both the prosthetic and the skin. Wait for it to become tacky—about a minute. Then position the prosthetic, pressing down firmly and holding it in place for 30 seconds.

- **Touch Ups:** I used to take a small bottle of glue with me for touch ups during a long con day. I haven't had to do that with Pros-aide adhesive.

My experience with making, painting and wearing latex prosthetics can probably help you as you start your journey, but is limited to the Seven of Nine costume.
So let's ask an expert in latex prosthetics!

EXPERT'S CORNER
by Rory Sunderland

My name is Rory Sunderland and I am a consultant with Harrison Designs and Concepts (HDC) Fabrication (info@hdcfab.com). I have worked closely with owner Timothy Harrison since 2012 designing cosplay props and fabrication projects for stage, screen, commercial and personal/pro cosplay. My full-time career is as a Cloud Automation Engineer/Architect.
My hope is that this overview will be a primer that will provide some sound information for beginners and help you move on to the next step.

Create and Apply Latex Prosthetics

Materials:

- Silicone (preferred for flexibility and lifelike flesh, but $$) or
  Flexacryl (preferred for stiffer parts like finger extensions, bone $$) or
  Liquid latex (low-budget, simpler build, easy to paint/blend)
     -(tinted to approximate skin tone preferred to save steps)
     -(start with small volume test to ensure you don't have latex allergies)

- Sculpting clay, Mold, or Item you'd like to replicate for your prosthetic

- Breathing protection for mold release sprays or paints

- Adhesive (order of preference):
  Pros-Aide (strong, not coming off till you take it off) OR
  Graftobian Pro Adhesive (very good, very near equivalent to Pros-Aide, and my go-to)
  Ben Nye Prosthetic Adhesive (I've used on sensitive skin and works very closely to Pros-Aide quality)
  Spirit Gum (can be effective for short-lived wear, but releases eventually

with sweat)

- Alcohol-based cosmetic paints (Alcohol is my preference because it will not come off without makeup remover and blends well)

- NITRILE Gloves - Do not use Latex gloves! Latex and Silicone will not respond well with Latex gloves - Latex only bonds to Latex, and it bonds well!

- Face/skin cleanser

- Astringent

- Cosmetic sponges and cotton balls/swabs

- Translucent powder (Graftobian or Ben Nye Neutral Set)

- Optional -
  Mann Ease Release 200 spray
  Home-made release agent "on the cheap" with the following tested recipe: -Castor Oil (10%) A cap-full (this is plant-based and will not destroy latex) -Spray bottle
  -70% rubbing alcohol - 10 - 12 oz

EZ Mode build (Low-cost Latex method):

Start with a sculpt of your prosthetic from Monster Clay, a mold you've made, or an object you want to replicate (you will be applying a release agent and latex to this item so it will get "dirty").

NOTE: As mentioned above, your model/sculpt cannot be latex or silicone (depending on what you are using). The liquid latex will stick to latex and not release, ruining your prosthetic. Model should be clay, mold with a release agent, or a model with a release agent.

Spray release agent, if you have it, on the model/mold/clay you are replicating (this will allow you to easily remove the latex without damaging it).

If you can purchase colored liquid latex, try to find one that is a relatively close match to your skin tone.   Latex can be tinted easily with acrylic paints, but the challenge is that standard liquid latex goes from bright white to translucent yellow when dry, so target color will be significantly darker.

Apply thin layers of liquid latex to your model/sculpt. You can use a brush, disposable sponge or controlled pour.
If brushing/sponging, liquid layer should level out a bit before it dries to reduce the appearance of brush lines.
Use enough liquid to allow it to settle a bit.

Excess can be trimmed off at the end.

Start at the center mass of your model and work your way out.

Keep the edges that will attach to skin as thin as you can. This will allow the prosthetic to blend to skin easier when applied. Build up layer upon layer when the previous layer is dry or near-dry. (Drying time is typically 5-10 mins, can start new layer as early as 5mins) A hair dryer can be used on cool air setting, but there is a learning curve to dry times.

NOTE: When the prosthetic is at desired thickness and rigid enough for your liking, pay close attention to the surface of your last layer. This is what is going to show, so take your time on final layers to get the texture you want.

Applying the Prosthetic:
Thoroughly clean the area of skin where the prosthetic will be applied. For best results, use some astringent with a cosmetic sponge or cotton ball on skin.

If joining directly to skin, position prosthetic (phone a friend if possible) and lightly mark the outline at key points with a slightly darker skin-tone (something easy to cover with final makeup).

Two approaches for attachment-
(TAKE YOUR TIME AND LINE UP CAREFULLY)

• Larger pieces - Keeping the prosthetic piece in place, lift sections and apply adhesive to the skin AND the piece within the area you've marked, allowing the adhesive to dry to tacky. Roll the prosthetic piece onto the skin slowly to avoid bubbles or gaps.

• Smaller pieces - Remove the prosthetic piece and apply adhesive to both skin and piece where it will attach. Once the adhesive is "tacky", start with one end of the prosthetic, aligned with marks on skin, and roll onto skin from along curve of skin (top to bottom,etc. as preferred).

Let adhesive to cure a bit; a hair dryer on "cool" can reduce drying time. Check seams where the prosthetic attaches to skin. Use a wedge sponge or q-tip and apply a thin layer of adhesive along the seam where skin and prosthetic meet. When adhesive dries, do this at least 3 more times so the dried adhesive fills the gap. You can use alcohol and a q-tip to "blend" thin edges of the latex to your skin to make the seam near invisible.

SEAL the prosthetic:
Using a light coat of adhesive, you can coat and seal the prosthetic so paint colors will dry evenly. If the prosthetic is not sealed, it will absorb the paint and affect blending. Use translucent powder on the prosthetic to make it ready for paint and remove any tackiness. Check surface lightly with finger to remove any remaining tacky areas.

Painting the Prosthetic:

I find alcohol-activated paints are most effective here and they are safe, even on thin bald caps. Alcohol-activated paints will last, are easy to blend, and will not come off with sweat or water.

NOTE: ***Avoid use around sensitive areas like the eye socket or nostrils.

Use skin safe cosmetics to blend these delicate areas.

Start with skin-tone blending first, and then work in various colors in a palette. Solid colors will not look "real". Include imperfections, bruises, freckles, etc.

You can "flick" the brush bristles for a random spatter effect (freckles/blood) or use a sponge to blend colors.

Example of an extensive facial prosthetic utilizing all the techniques laid out here:

Reference:
Stan Winston School is credited as the source for some of my information, backed by personal experience.
Stan Winston is widely regarded as one of the go-to industry experts for film, television, and advanced makeup/prosthetic design.

Person of note for Stan Winston lessons: Creature FX master Bruce Spaulding Fuller (PREDATOR 2, TERMINATOR 2, ARMY OF DARKNESS)

Note: If you are serious about industry work with prosthetic applications or a serious cosplay designer, I highly recommend supporting Stan Winston School and experiencing the training first-hand.

Photographer: Robert Remme

Chapter Ten

Getting Ahead of the Costuming Game
Wigs, Hairpieces, Headpieces

Wigs, hairpieces, and headwear have the power to be the cherry on the top of your cosplay creation. Knowing techniques for styling and attaching them is crucial for achieving your desired look, and can avoid a midday emergency in an overheated convention hall.

In this chapter, we'll explore useful tips for styling, and securing these hair accessories, as well as how to avoid slippage, that famous "wig shine" and oh, so many snarls.

I've utilized wigs in a number of costumes; Jean Harlowe, Cersei Lannister (both long and short), Starbuck, and most recently Siren Maya. I'll get into a few here.

The long Cersei is a standard cheap blonde wig, but has stood up to years of needing to be brushed and brushed again. I always start from the bottom and work in sections to avoid pulling the synthetic hair out (as much as possible). I ended up trimming the Starbuck wig to achieve the right length and style, and then used hair gel to get a separated, somewhat greasy look. I have used dry shampoo on wigs to knock down the "synthetic shine" with some success, though some dry shampoos can leave a greyish residue that shows up more on dark hair colors.

The Siren Maya wig was sort of an experiment, as I didn't know how short I could make the hair without having the weaving pattern in the back of the wig show. I separated the long front sections and kept them clipped out of the way, cutting a bit at a time around the sides and back to avoid taking too much off at once. The end result was not bad, though I didn't achieve the geometric cut that the character has. I'm not a hairstylist, though, so I'm giving myself some grace. A handheld vacuum was priceless in keeping little bits of synthetic hair from being on every surface and in -every- crevice for days.

But is it Eeeevil Hair?

I've also used synthetic hair to create headpieces/hairpieces for a number of costumes, the most extravagant being the hairpiece for the Evil Outfit of Evil (front cover). For this hairpiece I incorporated two synthetic reddish brown ponytail falls, and two longer red-to-black ombre hair falls.

I used the ponytail falls as the base, stitching them together with heavy matching thread from beneath. The red falls I used on either side and down the back, twisting the hair around each other to create swirls and stitching those down with "invisible" thread.

Since the red falls are separate from the brown, I was able to leave a gap to wiggle in my giant horns, which are attached to a headband. With this headpiece, many large bobby pins really do the heavy lifting in keeping it secure.

For headbands, hats I've made, and even crowns, I've had luck with the technique of attaching a short length of ribbon to the inside of the hat/headpiece at both sides, and sometimes in the back, on the inside where a hatband would be. On a bakeable clay crown I made, I glued the ribbon edges, while leaving a gap in the middle. The purpose of these ribbons is to secure it via bobbi pins.

Styling Tips

- *Customization:* I cut 90% off the wig I purchased for my Maya costume, and used a temporary hairspray to add a bit more color to the tips. My advice is, cut less than you think you need to. Stop and try it on. Go slow. You can always cut more.

- *Heat Styling:* If you have a synthetic wig, be cautious with heat styling tools, as many synthetic fibers can't withstand high temperatures. Human hair wigs can generally be styled with heat, but always use a heat protectant to prevent damage.

- *Think Ahead:* If you can avoid it, try not to do a lot of styling or brushing of the wig while it's on your head. It can pull at your wig cap, and it's much easier to style the back when you're not wearing it. A styrofoam wig head is great for styling or storing(you can tape or pin the wig to it)!

Attaching and Securing Wigs

- **Prep Your Hair:** Make sure your hair is secured to avoid edge escapees. For longer hair, consider braiding or using a wig cap to flatten your hair against your scalp. My favorite braid technique is two french braids all the way down the sides, and then the ends secured across each other. I like this because it's still cute when you take off the wig, whether you leave the braids in or let your locks loose.

- **Use Adhesives Wisely:** For most wigs, bobby pins are enough to secure a wig for me. I use a couple criss-crossed under the wig edge at the temples, and a couple more on each side of the nape of my neck. With lace front wigs, you may want to use a glue at the hairline. Again, I have to recommend Pros-Aide, but you should always do a test patch with glues. Same as with applying prosthetics, let the layer of glue become tacky before you press the wig onto it.

- **Opera Style:** This is the process described to me by the wiggist for the local opera company. Prep your hair for the wig cap (such as a bun or braid). Put the wig cap on, pulling it about ½" back from your hairline. At your upper and lower temple, on each side, use a small comb to pull out a small amount of hair from behind the cap. You will be wrapping these around a finger to make a curl that will lie, tight against the edge of the wig cap, and you'll crisscross two small bobby pins over the curl. You will do the same with two small bunches of hair at the nape of your neck on either side, one higher up behind your ear, and the other closer to the base of your skull. This technique keeps your wig cap VERY secure, so you can secure your wig over it, and it will not shift or pull back from your hairline.

Don't!

- **Let It Go:** When you're done wearing your wigs or headpieces, take care of them- return them to the original condition by styling or brushing before you put them away, or wash them (usually handwashing with a gentle soap) if they were exposed to dirt or sweat.

- **Too Hot to Handle:** Excessive heat can lead to damage, it can even start melting synthetic wigs surprisingly quickly.

My own experience with wigs and hairpieces has been varied, across a handful of costumes. My tips will surely help, but....
let's ask an expert for their advice!

Stephanie Schultz

Stephanie Schultz is an artist and apparel designer based in Milwaukee, WI, specializing in historically influenced high fashion. She meticulously research-es for each collection or high-concept project to produce a cohesive narrative around a subject, intentionally creating each ensemble with the purpose of storytelling. Involved in this process is of course coordinating the perfect hair, makeup and headpiece!
Her work can be found at Silversärk.com.

Tips for Securing hair:

Split your hair in half down the center, starting at the forehead and working towards the base of the skull.

Take the right side, and starting at the scalp, gather the hair and twist it, working down to the tip of the hair until it is rather tight (but not painful.)

Using bobby pins, secure the hair in place starting from the base of the skull and working towards the forehead and back around to the base of the skull, basically creating a circlet of twisted hair pinned down at the hairline.

Take the left side and do the same process, except securing it in a spiral pat-tern around the crown of the head.

Then apply a wig cap (a fishnet one is preferred, as it is easier to poke bobby pins through down to the hair and scalp.) This creates a great base to not only keep the hair down after the fishnet wig cap is on, but also provides a sturdier base for more bobby pins if wearing a particularly wiggly headpiece that requires more security.

Tips for Securing Wigs:

Items like "socks glue" or other roll-on body adhesives are a great way to keep a wig in place if there is significant weight or pulling happening to the hairline with styling or headgear.

However, this product does tend to remain a bit tacky after drying, so only apply to the exact area to be glued down. This product is easy to clean and does not stain. It is also practical for keeping thigh-highs and gloves in place, or any areas with lots of friction/clothing movement. It is less likely to adhere well in cold environments, but is easier to use than Spirit Gum.

Secure the wig in a few key areas around the crown and hairline with bobby pins the same color as the wig, so the bobby pin reaches the hair under the wig cap.

Tips for Securing Headpieces:

Be a cheater – headpieces will stay on better with an anchor that goes around the entire circumference of the head. Elastic cord is a great choice as it hides easily under longer hair & can be pinned in place to hair/wigs.

Cut a length of elastic cord, knot each end, and tack it to the inner sweatband of the hat (or where a sweatband would be on a lined hat) at the coronal mid-point of each side of the hat. If sewing is not an option, E6000 is the next best thing, and works best with a setting time of 24 hours and mini binder clips.

If the aesthetic allows it, hat pins function as a fashionable and sensible form of hat-fitting. Vintage and antique hat pins that are at least 10" long are a great way to keep a hat in place at anchor points the elastic cord is not able to secure. I personally use elastic to anchor at the temples and around the hairline to the nape, and a large hat pin across the mid-scalp region.

Examples of my work with wigs, hats and headpieces:

Chapter 10 Cover Model: Laura Meyer
Expert's Corner images provided courtesy of Stephanie Schultz

Chapter Eleven

All the Colors of the Rainbow
Dyeing Fabric

Have you tried dyeing fabric?
I did, and naturally it was for a big project that I absolutely could *not* mess up on.

Cuz that's how I do.

This chapter will take you through the process, and the in's and out's, of fabric dyeing.

It was a new project. I had eight yards of a striped fabric in a French blue-grey, or "brey", color, but I wanted a darker blue for the planned dress. I was going to dye it but I wasn't sure of the fabric content, and that can affect not only the type of dye you use, but the results you'll get. The stripe on the brey fabric was a cut pile velvet,and I was pretty sure it would be a different fiber than the base fabric.

A burn test indicated the stripe with the pile was 100% cotton, while the twill base was a blend of two fibers. Because of this, I knew the results with any dye would yield a two-tone blue, which could work for the project. But I'd never dyed a large (or any) amount of fabric before, so there was some learning to do.

Ending the suspense: the before & after.

Fabric Types
For those first entering the arena of fabric dyeing: the fiber content of your fabric WILL determine what type of dye you'll use & how well it will work. Natural fibers take dye more easily, as it soaks into the fibers.

The most common natural fibers include cotton, wool, linen, bamboo and rayon (surprised?). Rayon is a reprocessed cellulose fiber (wood) so it takes dye as well as cotton. But use care; when it's wet it's weak and vulnerable to tearing.

Synthetic fibers are generally more difficult to dye because the dye must stain the surface of the fibers. The most common synthetic fibers are polyester, nylon, spandex and acrylic.

Dyes for synthetic fibers may require the fabric to be boiled with the dye. This is another reason it's important to know your fiber content; some fabrics would be completely ruined if you tried boiling them, and some will barely be affected by a dye in water that's not hot enough.

You can burn a (very) small sample of the fabric in question with a lighter to help determine the fiber content. Generally speaking, natural fibers will burn down to ash and synthetics will melt, leaving a hard plastic-like nub behind. Specifics of this test are easy to find online.

The Chemistry

Once you know what type of fabric you have (get a pic of the information on the bolt or website for later reference) and what dye you'll use, you need to figure out how much dye to use to get the color you want on your fabric.

Generally, dyeing natural fiber fabric requires adding dye and salt to hot water, wetting your fabric thoroughly, immersing the wet fabric in the dye bath and stirring it constantly for at least 45 minutes to two hours… the longer it soaks, the more vibrant your color will be.

Making the magic happen- wear gloves!

To my credit, I did 3 tests with squares of the fabric in a cup of hot water, and tracking the results from using varying amounts of dye. My KitchenAid mixed each sample for an hour. That's me, working smarter, not harder! (Please note, if you use a stainless steel pot/tools, make sure to scrub them with a bleach cleanser/powder after using them for the dyeing process, as recommended by RITdye. Otherwise, do NOT use them for food again!)

I ended up with three swatches which gave me a pretty good idea of what my baseline results would be. My burn tests indicated that there was a higher cotton content in the raised fuzzy stripes than in the background weave, so the stripes absorbed a little more of the dye. The fabric

71

would be slightly two-toned, but still pretty monochromatic. My hope was that this would lend some depth the color and actually be a good thing. I discovered a few options online for how to dye large amounts of fabric: in large plastic bins, in stationary tubs, or in washing machines.

The Dye Bath

I chose to dye my fabric in two batches in the stationary tub in my basement. Why two? If the fabric is cramped and doesn't have the room to move freely as you stir, you can end up with uneven spotting. So I pre-washed my fabric (unwashed fabric can have chemicals in it that could affect the dye, but prewashing also means any shrinkage happens before you cut into the fabric) and cut out the pattern pieces so I'd have less to dye.

Note- it's a good idea to serge or zig-zag the edges of those cut pieces at this point so you don't lose your seam allowances to fraying during the whole dyeing and drying process.

For my outfit, the skirt of course included much more material than the jacket- and my dye amount calculations were based on fabric weight- so I put the center skirt pattern piece in with the jacket fabric to even out the weight between the two batches.

Ugghhh...

Resist the urge to toss in the last bit of dye in the bottle because you don't want to waste it, or because this load is a little bit bigger, or for whatever reason; if you did your calculations, the dye amount you use should be correct and more dye will just alter your results.

I did that.
It altered my results.

The center of my skirt was just a little lighter than the rest. I redesigned the skirt to break up the blue panels, but I could have avoided that if I'd just stuck to my dye recipe. Please, learn from my mistakes, that's why I wrote this book!

Smaller projects: Before & After

A less bright green for Starbuck pants called for dark blue dye.

I needed a darker, less yellow gold, so used brown RIT dye.

Tips for Dyeing Fabric

- **On using washing machines to dye fabric:** If you'd like to use a washing machine you'll have to be present to continually reset it to the agitation mode- you don't want it going to "rinse cycle" after 20 minutes! You may need to scrub/bleach the inside of your machine afterwards as well.

- **SALT:** Salt will help your fabric to accept the dye more easily. General consensus is 1 cup of salt per gallon of water.

- **Water:** You need to wet your fabric thoroughly before putting it into the dye bath. Thoroughly. Did I mention thoroughly?

- **Heat:** You need to use the hottest water you can get out of your tap (and even hotter for some fabrics/dyes; make sure to read the bottle). I turned the water heater up for several hours before starting, just so I could get more heat. This also helps the salt dissolve into the water.

- **Movement:** You NEED to keep your fabric moving during that 1-2 hour stirring session. I turned on a movie & kept the fabric going with a long wooden spoon.

- **Gloves!:** You need heavy vinyl/rubber gloves. The dye will stain your hands faster than it'll dye cotton! Do yourself a favor and wear old clothes when you're dyeing fabric, too.

- **MOAR water:** You need to rinse the dye out of your fabric at the end of the dye bath until it runs clear, or very close to clear. This WILL take a long time, but you don't want your fabric staining other clothing or your skin the first time you wear it.

My first big dyeing project, for the Vivienne Gown, and the other smaller ones after that, have turned out pretty well, so my tips are a great place to start....but let's ask an *expert*!

Expert's Corner

Dyeing to Cosplay
By Lyndzi Miller

Sometimes you need that perfect shade of fabric, yarn, or fiber and the stores just don't have it, buying online is risky, or you already have a perfect garment for the cosplay, it's just not the right color.

In those instances, dye can be your savior (or your nemesis, if you're not careful!). Here are some tips I have acquired from almost two decades of dyeing yarn for my geeky yarn shop, Lady Purl Designs, and dyeing fabric and costume pieces for my various cosplays over the years. I've

ruined countless items and wasted a ton of time so you don't have to!

Things you may need:

- Pot, metal tub, or bucket (used only for dyeing)
- Drop Cloth (to protect surfaces)
- Dye
- Fiber, fabric, or garment
- Gloves
- Metal tongs or spoon (used only for dyeing)
- Salt (for cotton or linen)
- Vinegar or Citric Acid (for wool or silk)
- If you're doing natural dyeing you'll need the colorant (like onion skins, turmeric, or beets)

Dyeing can be done in a pot on the stove or in a bucket (dyeing wool needs to be hot and dyeing cotton can be cold), or you can hand paint the dye onto the fabric (like tie-dyeing), depending on the effect you're looking to accomplish. If you want one solid all-over color or a more variegated/multi-color look, your process will differ.

Ready your workspace and read your dye's specific directions (instructions will usually be on the box, jar, or dye container).
Each brand is going to have different specifications for how much to use (usually the amount is relative to how saturated you want the color to be), how long to let it sit (again, less time usually ends up with a lighter color), and how hot or cold the water needs to be.

Different dyes work for different fabrics, so figure out the fiber content of your material to make sure you have a dye that will work for it. Some brands, like RitDye, are a mixture of different types of dyes with the hope that it will work on any material. The brand of acid dye I use for wool yarn will not work on plant fibers like cotton at all, and the dyes I have for cotton yarn will at most stain animal fibers like wool or silk.

Natural dyeing can be cheap and effective but is often unreliable. Beets can create a vibrant purple color or look like a red wine stain; turmeric can make a beautiful gold or a burnt brownish beige. It all depends on the fabric, so testing is a good thing to do if you really care about the fabric or garment you're hoping to dye.

Use a drop cloth to protect any surface you don't want dye splattered on because it inevitably will splatter. Pre-soak your material for a more even dye. If there are parts of the material that are dry, the dye won't

penetrate that section and will look streaky. You can soak the fabric for a few hours or overnight to make sure it's soaked through, but if you're in a hurry you can massage the fabric underwater to make sure every inch is wet. You can test out the dye color by dipping a corner of a paper towel into the dye pot and seeing what color it turns. Wet fabric will always look darker, so keep that in mind.

Dried, the fabric will always be a shade or two lighter. This is particularly important if you want blood red and it turns out pink or you want black and it turns out gray. For dyeing wool yarn, I always seem to need more red and black dye to avoid getting pink or gray.

Keep the fiber moving in the dye pot to avoid streaks. If using hot water, you can let the fiber sit in the water to soak up every drop of dye while the water cools. It will also be much safer to handle once the water has cooled down. Once the dye has been soaked up and the water looks clear, wash the fabric until the water runs clear. If it keeps leaking dye, it may be that the dye did not set properly and you'll want to set it with salt, vinegar, or citric acid, depending on the fiber content.

Once dyed, I recommend you wash the piece by hand, or in a machine with like colors, or even completely separately for the first few times after dyeing, just in case the color bleeds. If you want to wash the fabric in your washing machine, use cold water and wash it on its own. Afterward, it's a good idea to run your machine on a heavy load with hot water and a cup of bleach to clean it out, especially if you're worried about lingering dye in the machine.

Dyes are sold in hundreds of different colors, from "flamingo pink" to "radioactive acid green," so if there's a specific tone of color you have in mind, it probably exists. If you don't want to have a hundred-pot dye collection, you can make your colors with some color math and dyeing guides. They'll usually read something like: "Mix 1tsp Bright yellow and 1tsp Vermillion to get Persimmon Orange," or "Mix 1tsp Aqua and 1tsp Forest Green to get Teal." All colors break down into some variant mixture of red, yellow, and blue, but just using those may make you want to rip your hair out. Alternatively, if you only need teal dye, buy teal dye.

For a more speckled dyed look (great for hand-dyed yarn, not the best for fabric you want to look like a solid color), or if you want your fabric to look dirty/ blood-splattered, you can sprinkle powdered dye on the wet fiber and let it sit. Do not mix it or agitate it, the wet fiber will soak up the dye and stain darker in the spots where the dye sits.

The Rit brand has a dye remover powder, which can be very helpful if you want a lighter color, or if you make a mistake. It happens to the best of us.

Be safe and happy dyeing!

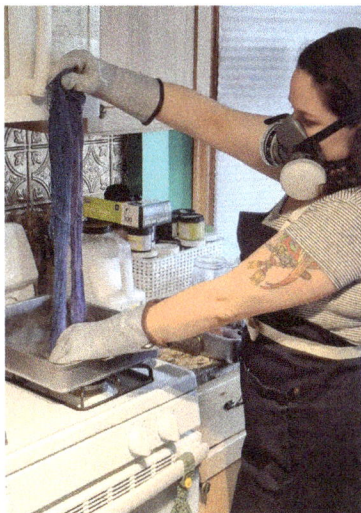

Safety Warnings:

Anything you use to dye should be used only for dyeing.

Most dyes are toxic (except natural dyeing methods), so you should not use the same pot for dyeing as you do for food. If you want to save money, get an old pot and metal tongs from a thrift store and use them strictly for dyeing.

Make sure to wear gloves. These dyes will stain your skin. Cover the rest of your body in old clothes and shoes too, while you're at it, because dye baths have a knack for splashing and ruining things. I have learned this the hard way! If using powder dyes, be sure to wear a mask.

Don't use powder dyes around open containers of food or uncovered drinks. If you have a cup of coffee nearby, you will more than likely see little dots of pigment in the cup after dyeing, even if it's sitting across the room! If you need a beverage nearby, make sure it is covered or closed.

Lady Purl process

Lady Purl product!

Chapter 11 Cover Models: Laura Meyer & James Opalewski
Expert's Corner images provided courtesy of Lyndzi Miller

Chapter Twelve

I Hate Sand(ing)
Prepping 3D Pieces for Painting

"It's a learning experience. It's a learning experience."

That's the mantra I kept telling myself as I sat down, staring at the plethora of 3D printed Bo Katan armor pieces scattered across my workbench.

If you've ever worked with 3D prints, you know that the real work isn't in the printing—no, that's just the beginning. The challenge comes when you're faced with raw, unfinished pieces that need time, attention, and a lot of elbow grease to transform them into something worthy of a Mandalorian.

So, buckle up, because in this chapter you're diving with me into the messy, satisfying, and occasionally frustrating journey of preparing Bo Katan's armor for painting.

Spoiler alert: It's not for the faint of heart, but end result is totally worth it.

The Bo Katan Kryze costume had been knocking around in my brain for about a year as a possibility. That spring, I was talking with a friend who was just a little obsessed with 3D printing about how the making of the armor was going to be a huge unknown as far as my existing skill sets go. Whether I chose to try 3D printed pieces or foam, I had no experience in either area. And I love a challenge.

Well, my excitement got him excited, and before I knew it we'd struck up a deal that he'd print the armor if I found the patterns. I actually found a reputable seller online, an Etsy seller with a solid reputation and a page of positive reviews longer than Bo's list of enemies.

I double-checked that the patterns were what he needed, bought them and sent them along. And then I waited.

The 3D Prints Arrive

The first step is deceptively simple. After waiting some months for the prints to arrive (because everything in cosplay seems to take longer than expected), I was finally holding the base pieces of Bo Katan's armor: chest plates, gauntlets, thigh guards, shin guards... the whole nine yards. I'd get

the back plate, helmet and jetpack later, but that was MORE than enough to get started! They were all fresh out of the printer, and while they looked great from a distance, up close, they were covered in all the telltale signs of 3D printing—layer lines, rough spots, and a few random imperfections.

Now, don't get me wrong—3D printing is a fantastic way to create intricate costume pieces, and the prints were solid. But 3D prints need work. And by "work," I mean I was about to embark on a journey that involved sanding, filling, smoothing, and yes, even a little cursing along the way.

What I Used:

Before I dove in, I made sure I had my toolkit ready. Here's a quick rundown of what you'll need if you ever find yourself in this same boat:

- Sandpaper (various grits): You'll need a mix, but I started with 100-grit for the big stuff, and worked my way up to 400-600-grit for wet sanding.

- Evercoat Polyester Glazing Putty (body filler): Wow. This stuff is your best friend when you need to fill in gaps or imperfections. It's strong, easy to apply, and it sands down like a dream. I'd say it's expensive, but you're only buying it once, and the amount of work it saves is priceless.

- Primer: I used Rustoleaum's automotive filler and sandable primer. When possible, it can be a good idea to use the same brand as the paint you choose, to be sure they work well with each other.

- Painter's tape: Because even Mandalorian armor isn't immune to paint mishaps.

A place to work: If you're lucky, you may have, or have access to, a spray booth with a fan. I am not that lucky, so I set up a make-it-work spray booth in my backyard (still using an N95 mask, btw), hanging old sheets up on three sides of a popup tent to protect the interior from any breeze-driven debris. If you plan to set up a place inside PLEASE make sure you have adequate ventilation for sanding and spraying, and a really good mask/ventilator.

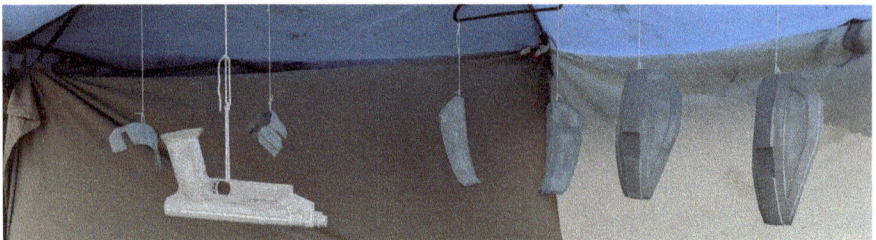

I present for your amusement, my sketch outdoor spray tent.
These leg pieces are final-coat primed and sanded and ready for the undercoat.

Sanding: The Great Equalizer

So, first things first. I grabbed some 100-grit sandpaper and started working on those layer lines. If you've ever sanded down a 3D piece, you know the feeling—the constant back-and-forth, the grainy buildup beneath your fingers, the impatient feeling of "this is going to take forever!"

It didn't take long for me to start problem solving… and I found the electric palm sander. That definitely helped with the wear and tear on the ol' body, but it still seemed like I was sanding for a long time, and getting pilling instead of dust at times. Yep, it was getting too warm. I had to move from one section to another, otherwise the friction would overheat the plastic. Then I was concerned about taking too much of the surface plastic off… I know it's a plastic shell with an interior gridwork, and I didn't want to risk breaking through that shell.
Enter my hero…

Filling Gaps: "Bondo" to the Rescue!

I had hesitated due to the price, but that amount of sanding was wearing ME down, rather than the armor. So I got the Evercoat Polyester Glazing Putty, and my life changed. It is SO sandable. I essentially used it to fill in the gaps, but also where the printing lines were egregious. And suddenly I was making progress! I finished the leg pieces, the headband, the guns. I did work in small batches because the putty requires a two-part mixing process with the Evercoat Blue Cream Hardener. I used paper plates and popsicle sticks for mixing and application, and didn't have any problems. Remember… ventilation!

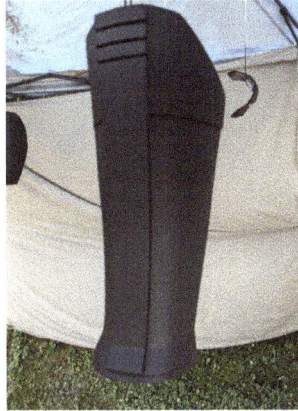

Priming—The Foundation for Painting
Once the sanding and filling were complete, it was time to get serious about prepping for paint. Primer is crucial, especially with 3D printed plastic, because it provides a surface for the paint to stick to. Without primer, your paint job will end up looking like a mess—so trust me, take your time here.

I laid down a couple light coats of primer, spraying it from about 6–8 inches away from each piece. The key is to apply thin, even layers— no heavy spraying. I let each coat dry fully before adding another. After the final coat of primer, I gave everything one last check for any missed imperfections or spots that needed a bit more sanding.

Preparing 3D Printed Pieces for Painting

- Initial Cleaning: Before sanding, use a craft knife or flush cutters to remove structures and extra bits from the printing process.Clean the surface of the print with isopropyl alcohol to remove oils and dust. Repeat when you're done sanding is complete, to ensure it's clean.

- Filling Imperfections: You may want to utilize a filler like I did in the sanding process. Use a putty knife or popsicle stick to apply. You can sand after the brief curing time, and the finish is great.

- Sanding Grits: You'll start sanding at 150-200 grit, and moving on to finer grits (220, 400, and up to 600 grit) will smooth the surface further. 600 is for wet sanding (just using some water during the process, but it works! (more for surfaces that will be highly reflective, like metallics).

- Primer: Use a sandable primer specifically designed for plastics. Don't use too much- light coats will dry more evenly.

- Paint Types: Always check the compatibility of paints with PLA. Some solvent-based paints can cause warping or melting!

- Overheating While Sanding: If using a handheld sander, take breaks to avoid overheating the surface and possibly deforming your piece.

Understanding PLA Types

It's important to understand the basics of PLA types because some don't hold paint well, or are brittle and aren't a good choice for pieces being worn. Some will melt under the heat of the sun or from the wrong type of paint.

- *Standard PLA:* This is the most common type of PLA, easy to print & offers good detail, but it can be brittle and may not hold up well under stress.

- *PLA+:* PLA+ has better strength, flexibility, and durability, can be easier to sand and gives a better surface for painting.

- *Wood-Filled PLA:* PLA contains wood fibers, so sanding may reveal the wood texture and make it more difficult to get an even coat with paint.

- *Specialty PLAs:* Some glow-in-the-dark or flexible PLAs may not hold paint well.

But *my* advice on prepping 3D parts, while hard-earned, is based on this particular Mandalorian-focused adventure. So, let's ask an expert!

Timothy Harrison

Based in Chicago, Tim Harrison of Harrison Designs & Concepts has over 10 years of experience working in the film, TV, and commercial industry. He is also an adjunct professor at The Theater School of DePaul University, teaching multi-medium fabrication and design in addition to various master classes and workshops with trade-shows, comic conventions, and local IATSE branches. HDC specializes in custom prop design and fabrication, from strike-safe stunt props to hyper-realistic hero prop and costume pieces. From bespoke awards to unique props for commercial and film work, HDC is known for their fine detail work and a cinematic level of finishing with practical effects, sculpting, casting, foam smithing, leatherworking, 3D printing and scanning, rapid prototyping and more.

The key to a realistic-looking prop or accessory is your surface preparation, regardless of medium. There are many different types or 3D printing technologies and materials but taking the time to create that solid foundation is what will ensure your success in making plastic look presentable. A great paint job will only look as good as the preparation put into its canvas. The surface preparation steps I prefer were refined for fused filament fabrication (FFF) based printing using PETG and also mSLA/SLA resin printing but work for all materials.

Preparation for painting:

1. For the initial once-over, I dry sand everything with 80 grit sandpaper. I use mechanical sanders; saves on manual exertion. Milwaukee has a detail sander that blows a lot of other models out of the water.

2. After the 80 grit, I use the Evercoat two-part body filler to fill in large deficits. Be sure to use appropriate ventilation and protections, as this is strong. Once the filler cures, I sand everything with 150 grit.

3. Then it's time for the initial primer coat. I use a Devilbiss GPi HVLP spray gun for primer spraying. I use U-POL, a urethane-based high solids, high build, four-to-one primer. This is quite viscous out of the can, but you can use a reducer to thin it for more detailed objects while maintaining the benefits of a catalyzed primer. A rattle can equivalent to U-POL would be the filler primer from Rustoleum. The Rustoleum takes much longer to dry, and the sanding process is a little more gummy.

4. Once the filler primer sets, do a light dry sanding with 220 grit, where needed, just to even things out. I will wet sand 220-300-400 for metallic coats as there is a self leveling clear coat I spray after this that helps cut back on sanding, and to 600 for regular color paints.

Please note *that while I've mentioned some higher end tooling and materials, the same process and finishes can be achieved with hand sanding and rattle-can based paints you can find at your local hardware store. The biggest difference and advantage to the different tools and materials is the speed in which you can complete the process.*

Chapter 12 Cover Model: Laura Meyer

Chapter Thirteen

Only As Old As It Looks
Painting, Ageing and Weathering Effects

You'll notice something different about this chapter, and I'll end the suspense; this particular cosplay build is not done yet. It happens. A Bo Katan costume, in particular, can take years (or thousands of dollars) to put together, and I've committed to creating a lot of it using skill sets I'm learning as I go. The armor, the pistols, the belt and holsters… it takes time.

But you don't have to wait until it's *all* done to benefit from what I've learned!

So instead of the finished costume picture, we're getting hot and heavy into some detailed pictures of the painting and weathering I've done to date, including how I improved a store-bought foam armor set for my GoT Jaime Lannister costume. (pictured, left)

The finishing touches of painting and weathering can dramatically enhance the authenticity and realism of your costume pieces and props. This chapter will explore effective techniques for painting and weathering for results that bring your characters to life.

These final stages have been some of the most fun—and arguably the most rewarding—parts of this build so far, and I've already got a LOT of tips to help you along. It's easy to get carried away at this point because the painting is where the vision of your cosplay really starts coming to life.

So, let's dive into the real fun of this project: how I painted and weathered Bo Katan's armor to make it look like it had been through the ringer. Here's the lowdown, and some early lessons learned. But first-

Jaime's Armor

In this book I discuss the Jaime Lannister costume build across a few chapters, from the coat and scalemail in chapter five, to the chestplate/greaves in this chapter, to the leather bracers in chapter fourteen. This pair of costumes, Jaime and Cersei, went a long way in stretching some unused creative muscles, and learning some new skills. A foam Kingsguard armor build would be the next, ambitious step, but at the time I was looking for a "good enough" rather than "excellent replica" kind of look. So I purchased a foam "Roman soldier" chestplate and backplate armor set, and matching shinguard. They had lions on them, so that's a step in the right direction.

But they were pretty flimsy. I wanted to make them more durable, and a repaint would be in order as well. My first step was buying a few cans of Plasti-Dip spray, and I gave the armor a few coats on the inside and outside, allowing it to dry according to the instructions in between each coat. That nearly doubled the thickness, and gave me a good base for painting. I used a antique gold spraypaint as a base and did a lot of drybrushing over the darker areas in the same direction to get a brushed metallic look to the finish. The shinguards received a similar treatment. On all pieces, I replaced the thin ribbon ties with leather straps and buckles I cut from scraps and riveted on, increasing the strength with two rivets at each attachment point and an additional piece of leather on the back for reinforcement. It's not completely accurate to the series, but it works and is still highly recognizable as the character.

Bo's Base Coat

The leg armor was ready for paint.
I headed to one of our holdout local art supply stores, Blick, for the blue and grey paint. I did a LOT of comparing very similar blues for the armor. Was it too bright, too aquamarie, too cobalt? At last, I stopped agonizing over blues and chose one, figuring I'd be darkening and aging it anyways. Choosing the grey was easier; I got a medium grey and a light grey, and that was that.

You don't want to rush the application of the base coat—if you apply it too thick, you risk ruining all the hard work you did in prepping the pieces. And I recalled a tip to always check the nozzle before spraying, and to clean it right away after.

I was so careful.

I sprayed the thigh guards and pistols first- dark and light grey, respectively. The shin guards were the largest pieces in my first round of armor. I gave a little extra care with them, giving light even coats…. when I noticed the finish was grainy, almost pebbled! I panicked, I didn't understand what was happening. I checked the spray can, but the nozzle wasn't gummed up. I had shaken the cans the recommended amount of time. I ran inside and looked up the symptoms I'd observed…

To find out that I had been TOO careful. I sprayed from too far away, and the paint had started to dry as it was hitting the surface. FART. There was no way around it. I would have to sand down the shin guards. Again. When they say 6-8 inches away from the surface, they mean it.

That wasn't the only teachable moment… I had given the headband a couple of coats of dark grey, and a coat of sealer. I laid the cardboard it sat on carefully onto the table outside my makeshift spray tent, and went inside. My husband, upon getting home from work later that

afternoon, came in the back door and asked right off the bat, "Why is Bo's headband shaped like an S?" I sat up like a shot, "You're kidding, right?", and when he shook his head I RAN out the back door.

Sure enough, sitting there on the cardboard in the backyard, the headband had taken on a lovely gentle 'S' curve. I knew my mistake immediately. In my recent research regarding PLA and what types of paint to use, I had read that standard PLA has a melting point of around 170 degrees fahrenheit, and softens around 140. I had left it to dry in the sun, and the heat had started to warp it.

In fix-it mode, I had an inspired thought. I took the headband into the bathroom and turned on my hairdryer. With patience, and from several inches away, I slowly reheated the headband. When it started to become flex-ible, I molded it to my own forehead, holding it to where it would be once I made attachments. So that's a happy ending, because I achieved a better fit than I had originally, but I've read about full sets of armor left in sweltering cars… and discovered by their owners as shapeless hunks of plastic in their protective bags. Hundreds upon hundreds of hours (or dollars) gone in an afternoon. I learned *my* lesson in a very painless way, and I'm glad for that!

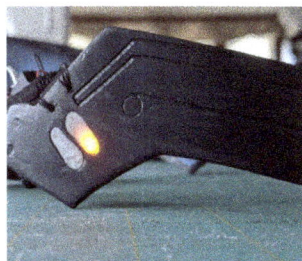

White hot glue and an LED is the first attempt for lighting the headband

The Magic of Weathering

Now, here's where things get messy—and in a good way. When I think of Bo Katan, I don't think of a clean, polished warrior. I think of someone who's fought in the trenches, worn their armor day in and day out, and still come out on top. I couldn't have her armor looking new. I used a couple techniques to weather it. One was airbrushing.

This was a pretty basic airbrush, but it was my first time using it. I tested it out on some scrap pieces of plastic to be sure I was comfortable with the use, pressure, and movement before using it on the armor I'd already spent so much time on. I used black, brown, even a dark yellow to get some realistic dirtiness. I started slowly, to avoid being too heavy handed with it.

I also used a black wash. A wash is a thinned-out paint that you apply to the piece and then wipe off, leaving only the paint in the recesses. This adds depth and shadows. I mixed black acrylic paint with a little bit of water to create the wash, then applied it with a sponge to the crevices of the armor. After a minute I used a clean, damp cloth to wipe away the excess. The result was a subtle, gritty effect. The armor looked like it had been through some serious skirmishes—and it wasn't done yet. The wash was better at getting into recesses- the airbrush paint mostly hit the surface areas.

Distress and Damage

Once the wash was dry, I began to add some damage to the armor. Bo Katan's armor, in particular, has visible signs of battle damage, from scuffs to dents to blaster burn marks.

I used dry brushing for some of this. I dipped a dry brush into a small amount of black paint, wiped most of it off onto a rag, and then gently brushed it over the areas where I wanted to add scuffs or scratches. I focused particularly on edges, making them look like they've been scraped or worn over time. I used a liquid metallic pen (and sometimes a dry brush or even a toothpick for application) to go over these black scuff areas, and give the look of the shiny metal of Bo Katan's armor, where the paint would have been worn away by the battle damage.

As I made the marks from "damage", I imagined her in battle- where would blows land? What direction would they be going? How would they hit the armor? I tried apply directional damage on the shins and thigh plates. The guns got more damage where they wouldn't be protected by hands or holsters, and it was also focused on wear along the edges.

For the pistols I was constantly referencing images of Bo's Westar 35's to figure out the right colors, shading, and areas for damage. I used the dark grey as an overall base coat and then taped off everything but the lighter areas, giving it a coat of the lighter grey. The grips I painted with a brown acrylic paint. They got some shading of recessed areas, and "scuffed" metallic highlights also.

I used a matte clear coat to seal my work… it took the shine down on the metallic paint, so I went back and did just a little touch-up over some of those shiny chrome highlights.

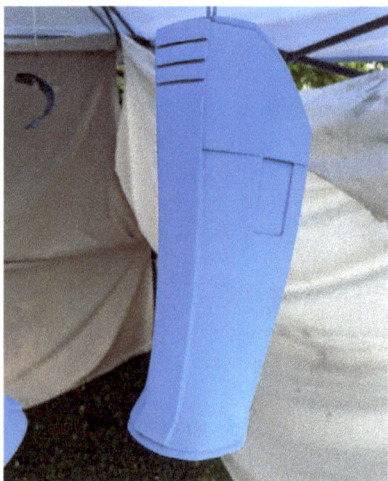

Color coat AFTER my oops.

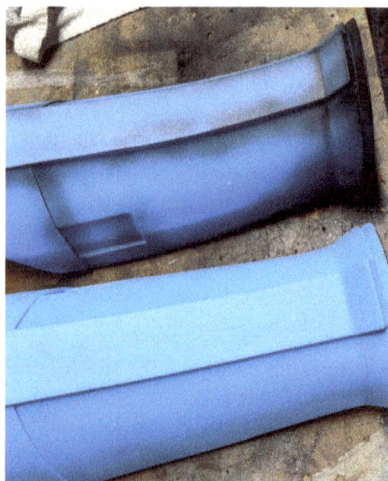

Before/after a round of air-brushing.

The Finished Product

I was pretty happy with the techniques I applied, and when I wore the armor to FanExpo in my Bo Katan/Starbuck mashup, I got some decent feedback from the folks at the 501st table. I think it can use a little more weathering, but I'll wait to do a final once over until ALL the armor IS at the same point. And that will need to wait until spring, because I don't have the ventilation to do this indoors. Below are images of the last stages of weathering/damage effects.

Tips & Techniques

- **Know Your PLA:** The type of PLA you use will inform your paint choices and more. For most materials, acrylic paints will work well to add depth and effects.

- **Base Coats:** Start with a solid base coat in a color that matches, or is darker than the overall color of your prop. Use a spray can for larger surfaces, but be sure to follow the instructions on the can for distance/timing of coats!!

- **Effects:** Dry Brushing, air brushing, or washes can add depth and character to the armor. Tutorials on these techniques are easy to find.

- **Heat Damage:** Be aware of the melting point of your PLA to avoid potentially disastrous discoveries.

- **Forgetting to Test:** Always test paints, washes, and techniques on scrap materials before applying them to your final piece, particularly if it's the first time you're using that material/paint/technique,

- **Fabric Wear:** For weathering and ageing fabrics, popular techniques include paint washes of diluted fabric paint or dye, air brushing in brown and gray colors, using a dremel tool or wire brush to create wear, or even mending or patching fabric to show that it is old or weatherbeaten.

After adding the metallic accents, I needed to go back and do some touchups.
Honestly I was happier with the paint job I did on the armor.

For my first time weathering armor/props, I learned a lot and got some good results. But there's so much *more* to learn, so....
let's ask an expert!

Expert's Corner

Timothy Harrison
Part 2

Painting is where you can dive in to develop a faux history for your prop or accessory and really shine as a visual storyteller. There can be a lot of prep and planning in this visual story development, or Chronosynthesis, as I like to call it, which is the act and art of emulating the passage of time.

When planning, I like to think about the environment the item comes from like a forest or industrial age or spaceships, old west, etc, the materials I'm trying to
emulate, what kind of weapon damage could be involved, like blade strikes, projectile weapons, plasma based weapons, laser based weapons, and so on. Has this been sitting in nature for decades or centuries? Is this a regularly worn item, or what kind of care does the person put into this item?

All of these factors take part in the color choices and textures I apply as they affect the choices or t ints, tones, or shades of base colors to emulate a warmer or cooler look based on the environment and history you're working to develop.

Just like anything else, you need a strong foundation to build on. Here are some of the steps I use to put that foundation in place and then get to the fun parts.
You want to start your painting process with a seal coat over the primer we talked about in the previous chapter. There are a few spray guns I named and each has a different purpose and specification but, as

mentioned before, everything can be done with locally sourced items and basic tool sets; it's just a difference in processing time.

The Step by Step Process

1. I use an Iwata LPH80 with a gravity cup for to spray my basecoat or seal coat. My base coat of choice is Createx Autobourne Black but I'll occasionally change the color depending on the final look I'm trying to achieve. A rattle can equivalent would be Bondo or Duplicolor Hot Rod black primer.

2. If working toward a metallic or chrome look, I'll spray the black seal coat after the 400 grit wet sanding. On the more complex side, if you're looking to achieve a pale chrome gold or an aged brass, you can base coat with a white or a red brown for some subtle tonal changes. Then I do an automotive gloss clear coat. My gloss clear of choice is Transtar 7761-MTR with the 6854 activator sprayed using a DeVilbiss GTI PRO LITE with a 1.2mm needle and T110 cap for catalyzed (2 part) clears.

There are fewer acceptable rattle can equivalents for this, in my opinion; I would use SprayMax Clear 2K Glamour. The benefit of using a gloss clear coat over a black base vs a gloss black or even black tinted clear coat is to help achieve more visual depth to create a more realistic metal base. Many of the chrome or metallic paints are partially transparent, so having that little extra bit of space for the paint to sit on above your black seal coat allows a bit more light bounce, which is what gives you a deeper, truer-looking metallic vs sitting directly on a black gloss base.

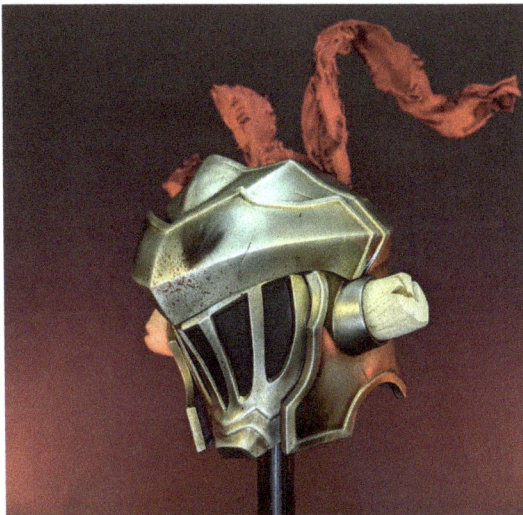

Replica Slayer Helmet

**Again, you'll need a solid respirator with cartridges to protect against organic vapors, acid gases and such like the 3M P100 Respirator Cartridge/Filter 60926 and very good ventilation to spray this stuff. If you like the process and spray regularly, I recommend a forced air fed, full face respirator.

3. For your paint colors after the 600 grit sanding, you'll do the seal coat and then the color base that you've chosen using the Iwata LPH80 again.

4. After that, for metallic armor you'll use Imperial Surface Alumaluster chrome paint and let things sit overnight.

5. Over top of that, spray the same gloss again to seal it after a very gentle buffing with a microfiber cloth. You can rush the topcoat application and spray your gloss right after the metallic coat but you do risk dulling your metallic if you're not careful.

While Alualuster is my goto and I feel it is the best at maintaining its brilliance post top coat, it is a higher end paint. Other options are Duralumen from Digital Armory on Etsy, Motostorm hypersilver or motochrome, alclad chome which needs additional steps to silver, and there is a newer rattle can option from Revell called Chrom (yes Chrom) Spray.

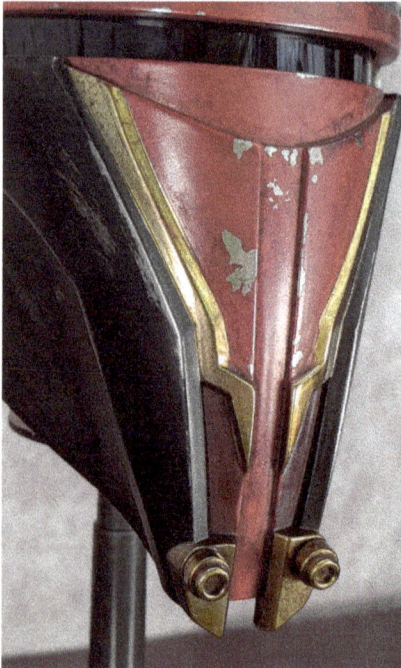

Darth Revan Helmet   *Mini Nuke*

6. Once you have your metallic or color base down or combo down, you can move on to your aging and weathering. I start with my washes, using a warm or cool tone based on my planning and then move to some finer pin washes with color variances to add that additional subtle detail. These would fall under your lowlights.

Then you can add highlights using dry brushing with metallic paints. I like Moltow Chrome pen refills or basic silver liquid leaf. In addition to metallic highlights, you can mix some gray or white to your base colors to apply tints to emulate sun bleaching and other color-fading highlights.

7. As you develop your skills with practice, you can add additive and subtractive damage textures with rotary tools, files, body filler stippling, cinnamon, and so much more.

Aged wood effect

Remember that the only thing that will prevent you from moving forward is not trying.

Embrace failures and learn from them. They are powerful tools to utilize when working with new methods and materials as they allow us to understand the breaking points of our work.

Once you have that understanding, it gives you the knowledge on how far you can push that process and what corners you can cut to help push a tight deadline or even land on a happy accident of a new way to achieve a specific look.

Chapter Fourteen

OMG Leather??
Project Planning with Leather Armor and Accessories

We've all been intimidated by an expensive fabric, a new skill, or an untried process.
Early in my sewing journey I was so intimidated by the thought of installing a zipper that I made my first skirt closure from velcro. It's true. I've had expensive or unique fabrics languish for years as I simmered in indecision over a project worthy of them.

"Oh, umm, leather?
I'd love to, but I don't have the machine to work on leather."

This is what I said for years, and I believed it.
I thought I needed a special sewing machine- an industrial machine- to handle the sewing of such a heavy material. Now I know that having the right needle and the correct thread makes it possible to sew leather on a wide variety of machines, including home use models.(Disclaimer, of course, that some machines are better suited than others to handle heavy materials and multiple layers of heavy materials!)

After that, my excuse was that leather is expensive. A fair point. However, when everyone in your immediate and extended circles knows that you can sew, fabrics tend to pop up. Years ago, a friend's friend was looking to get rid of a large bag of leather hides that had been sitting in an attic for a good while.

I received thirty pounds of leather and threw some money at them, they cleared out their attic, and we were all happy. I cleaned off a few mold spots, weeded out leather from pleather (there was one length in the pile), and separated out what I thought I might use.
I gifted the rest to a friend who was beginning to explore leatherworking and would certainly appreciate free pieces.

And then the leather, for the most part, sat there for another year, waiting for me to find a project worthy of it.
Or for me to overcome my intimidations.

This chapter takes you through my very first big leather project, blemishes and all.

A Warrior Is Born

At last, inspiration!

Having moved on from period Elizabethan gowns, I wanted to create more of a warrior look to wear at the Renaissance Faire. I found an image which evoked the feel I wanted, think "fantasy warrior meets battle-ready samurai", and I used that as a starting point for a tunic with leather armor panels.

At the start of this design I wasn't sure just how it would go together and I wanted to be prepared. I acquired some special supplies; heavy needles for my sewing machine and some leather hand sewing needles, an edge burnisher and black edgecoat, and heavy thread.

Before taking any steps with the leather, I created a knee-length tunic from a pebbled burgundy wool to serve as the base for the armor. I had a few yards of silk in the brightest orange you could possibly imagine, and I decided to dye it (see chapter 11) and then use it for the lining. I made sure the tunic was fitted and without stretch, as the leather going on top of it would not stretch either. I took measurements off a shirt that fit well, and made a pattern like an extended tank top. The sides angled out in an A-line. Precise fitting wouldn't be necessary as the tunic would close down the front, and be split from the waist down at the sides and back.

Once the tunic was complete, I used sheets of butcher paper to create a pattern for the armor plates, starting by tracing out the shapes with the paper pinned onto the tunic. Then I added an inch onto the top and bottom of each armor piece, accordingly, to allow for overlap. I considered how I would be moving in the tunic when deciding how to lay the pieces.

I referenced images of suits of armor to see where they allowed for extra movement.

I used an inexpensive upholstery pleather to cut out test pieces and see how they worked together, and once I was happy with the fit and placement, I (holding my breath) cut out the pieces from the actual leather.

Yes, I still messed up, very carefully cutting out two left shoulder pieces instead of a left and a right. There is such a thing as TOO much focus, it seems. Fortunately, I had extra leather and could cut another piece. I used foam tipped applicators to carefully

Figuring overlap.
Paper pattern pieces at top right.)

apply black edgecoat to each piece of armor plate. The key there was not to put *too* much edgecoat on the applicator at once.

With my leather plates ready, it was time to attach them to the tunic. This was where things could either go terribly wrong or look amazing – I knew I needed to take my time.

I started by laying the tunic flat on a table and positioning the plates where I wanted them to go. The plates were arranged in a vertical row on the front and back of the tunic, with each one overlapping slightly with the next.

The completed front of the tunic.

I carefully marked where each rivet would go, making sure to line up the edges of each plate perfectly, with about an inch of overlap. Using a hole punch, I created small holes in both the leather and the fabric. Then, one by one, I inserted the rivets and hammered them in place, creating a firm yet stylish attachment.

The rivets were spaced evenly, creating a visual rhythm down the front and back of the tunic. With each rivet that went in, the final look started to come together, like puzzle pieces clicking into place.

Once the plates were all attached, I took a moment to try the tunic on. It fit beautifully—the leather plates provided just the right amount of structure without making it too stiff, while allowing me full range of motion. After inserting pre-drilled steel bones at the front opening, I had debated what to use for the actual front closure of the tunic. I originally wanted several curved latch metal fasteners. However, in practice, the fasteners were not very stable and could come undone from too much movement- NOT great for battle. I created a center set of grommets which would be tied, more traditionally, with a ribbon or leather lace, and would keep the fasteners above and below from jostling around too much. A workaround, to be sure, but once the fasteners were riveted in my options were limited.

The Results

The leather plates provide extra body to the tunic shape, and look great. The overlapping of the edges really makes them look useful, rather than decorative. I'm happy with it, even if I had a make-it-work moment with the closures. I plan to add leather braces and a pauldron at some point, to really beef up the look. (The cover picture is taken with a pleather pauldron I had laying around and modified for a SCA date.)

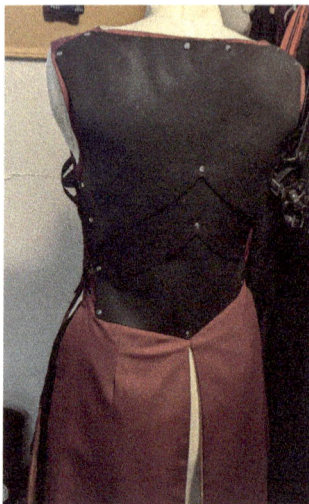

Not bad for a first go-around with a larger project.
Next to make some matching bracers!

Lannister Leather Bracers

A smaller leather project had led up to this one- making the bracers for the Jaime Lannister costume. They were leather, with overlapping gold scales, and a solid success. I had measured the wrist and forearm circumference of the cosplayer-to-be to draw up a pattern. Referencing online images, I figured out how big the "scales" should be to get the right look. Everything was cut out in paper first, because I didn't want to risk messing up and wasting leather.

I punched holes in the scales, and then used those holes to mark placement on the bracer base. I worked from the bottom up, as they overlapped, and used aged brass tone rivets to attach the scales to the base. Then I punched larger holes along the bracer's long edges, and put in grommets (not necessary with the thick leather base, but the Lannisters are *fancy*, so it seemed appropriate).

Tips for Constructing with Leather

- **Cleaning Basics:** My leather was obtained, for a steal of a deal, from a friend's friend's attic. I did some cleaning of potential problem spots when I first got it. If you need to clean leather, you can use cold distilled water, a mild soap solution, or a 50/50 solution of vinegar and water- but you should use leather conditioner on the piece afterwards to maintain its condition.

- **Mirror mirror:** Don't forget to flip your pattern pieces if you need a "left" and "right". (This is not a leather specific tip, it goes for any material that has a different pattern or surface on the opposite side!)

- **Measure Twice, Sew Once:** Once a hole is in leather, it is there to stay. Take your time to ensure you have as few "bonus" holes as possible!

- **The Clamp!:** Use small clamps instead of pins to avoid permanently marking your leather… and to avoid the painful death of your pins as you try to force them into materials they were never meant to experience.

- **The Clamp! 2.0:** Similarly to pin curl clips (there's a random topic shift!), you may still need to buffer the clamp with a small square of fabric to keep it from leaving an impression in the leather- it's always a good idea to test it first!

The Warrior of Indeterminate Origin looks great, and I feel it was a good first experience with a larger project using leather. However, for more in-depth process and planning tips, let's ask an expert!

Expert's Corner

The Dragon Spine
by Luke Milton

In 2014, I turned my passion for leatherworking into a full fledged business, growing from a one man hobby into to a 2 workshop 3 employee experiment I call 'House Of Wolfram'. I've dedicated my company to creating leather goods that find the meeting point of smart design and a luxury aesthetic. I'm also a cosplayer and most recently was able to play out some of my favorite anime characters from Final Fantasy and Castlevania for DragonCon 2024. For me, the real challenge, but also the real satisfaction is in the development and refining of a new, exciting design.

In my career as a leatherworker I've typically made smaller accessories; designing a large wearable piece is a risk in some ways, but the payoff

can be more than worth it. This chapter will take you through my process for designing what may be my favorite creation to date, the Dragon Spine.

Inspiration

Every designer finds inspiration in different places. The inspiration for the Dragon Spine came from the film "Alien" by Ridley Scott. I'm a huge fan of the movie, and the xenomorphs directly inspired the biomechanical aesthetic of the spine segments, reflected in the way the length of the leather "spine" ripples with movement along the entire body. I imagined a spiny column, starting high on the shoulders and hugging the curves of the back. To my surprise, there didn't seem to be anything similar available from other designers. It was so clear to me: one of those rare inspirational moments where you see the whole project worked out in your mind…
I couldn't resist drawing out a prototype.

The Design

I came up with a rough drawing and listing of the features. The spine segments would need some variation in size and shape as their purpose would change along the length of the body, just as they do in a real spine. I shaped them to be domed and then pointed, to evoke a classic dragon scale shape.
The principle for connecting the segments was drawn from the "leather link belt", a very old design in which many sections are folded over each other to make a flat chain. I added a hinge pin to connect the segments to each other, like a bike chain. Combining these two designs resulted in a more durable, segmented chain spine that was flexible in three dimensions.
An adjustable strap harness would attach in three places. The spine would move with the wearer, rolling over the shoulders, hugging the waist and swinging free from there. Just as important as adjustability was versatility; keeping the harness design simple would ensure it could be easily integrated with other costume pieces on many body shapes with minimal interference.

Leather options range from very soft and supple to extremely rigid; I wanted a leather stiff enough to hold its shape. I used a 2-3 oz cowhide,

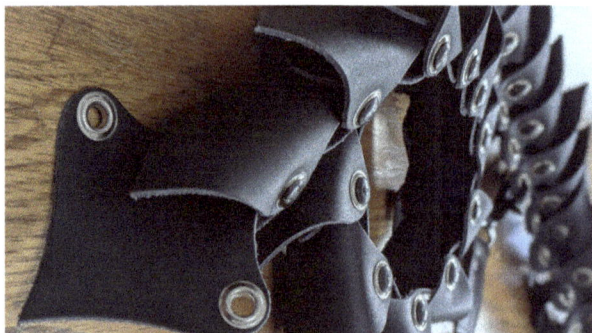

sturdy but not too stiff since I also had to bend it into the shape that would dome up on the pointed end. I chose a leather that was stamped and dyed to look like crocodile skin, for the lizard-like aesthetic of this particular project. Since then I have made Dragon Spines in many leather colors and patterns.

Patterning

The hardest part was designing the dimensions of the individual pieces. It can be paralyzing to try creating a shape from scratch, so I have a system to reduce difficulties. When patterning I start with the elements that are least changeable and use them as a baseline to "trial and error" my way towards the parts of the pattern that are more under my control.

Start With The Hardware

One element I often have little to no control over, and therefore start with, is the hardware. Working from the hardware outward in your design can ensure that the sizes and finishes you will need are readily available, and avoid the frustration of having to rework your design later, if you end up being unable to source a particular variation.

I begin by drawing up an example of what I want to make, making it as realistic as possible, and I make a list of all the hardware I can see it needing. Then I organize that hardware list by importance on a scale of "meh, I could probably sub that piece with something similar and it would still work" to "If I don't have exactly this piece exactly like this I need to completely redesign my whole concept".

Then I start researching.
When searching for your hardware options, prioritize finding function first, then aesthetics. Start on your hardware list, making sure your items exist in the sizes you need, and then take note of the color/finish options available. Use that as the baseline as you go down your list, taking notes on what is available in the same finishes, in case you need to go back with changes. This can be a long list; spreadsheets are a godsend.

The Principal Elements

The "principal elements" are aspects of the pattern that take priority over the aesthetics since they are necessary for the pattern to function. There are still aesthetic decisions to be made with the principal elements, though. For example, the segments need to fold over at the top to create a loop which will link the pieces together. It is a necessary element. However, as long as the foldover is there I can make it as wide, narrow, long, short, thick, thin as I want, guiding the aesthetics.
I then make a list of those elements and draw at least one rough shape that I think would satisfy those parameters just to get me started.

Keep in mind that there are probably a lot of very different shapes that would satisfy the parameters and this will be helpful when it comes to the aesthetics....you don't need to stick with one shape just because it was the first one you came up with.

Pure Aesthetics

Once my hardware options are laid out before me, and I have an idea of what roughly the shape should be to fulfill its functional requirements, I start adding real world measurements to the rough shape I came up with in step 2, using step 1 as a foundation.

For example, if a particular spot needs ½" grommets in a particular spot, I use the ½" grommet as a reference (since that part is fixed and unchangeable) and draw what the actual size of the shape would need to be relative to that grommet. Then I adjust the aesthetics of this shape however I like under these parameters until it starts looking like what I am envisioning.

Once I had the shape I wanted for the dragon spine segments, I scaled them to taper down the back, while making sure the size variations were still within the tolerances of the hardware. The segments of the top half were connected to each other via a binding screw secured with grommets. These act like a hinge which each segment is looped over, allowing the spine to flex, compress and expand in any direction without putting pressure on the piece.

The grommets which connect the ends of each segment also reinforce the holes which are the attachment points to the harness. This allows the harness to be attached on any segment for a perfect fit among different height and torso measurements. The grommets, large enough to fit the snap hooks of the harness, could also be used with standard rope for practical or decorative costume applications.

The bottom half of the spine served a different purpose, so the segments required a different shape. I designed segments that feel straight down like a tail, but still folded into the raised dragon scale point for integration with the top half. There was an issue to too much movement between the bottom segments that was absent in the upper half as they were flush against the body. I instead attached the top of each lower segment to the body of the following segment in a looping manner. This kept the flexibility but made each piece act more like a spring than a chain; moving one piece organically influences the movement of its neighboring pieces.

After spending about two frustrating weeks trying to figure out how to finish the tip of the tail, a happy accident resulted in the realization that leaving the bottom segment attached but unfolded looked absolutely perfect, and that I didn't need to do anything more to it after all. A great sigh of relief was uttered that day.

Finishing Details

After the design of the spine, the harness was easy. I wanted: simple, comfortable, low profile. I chose a soft motorcycle leather in medium thickness. I used 1 inch wide strips because 1 inch hardware is widely available in the US. The shoulder straps had simple tri-glide adjusters similar to bra straps, ending in snap hooks to attach

to the triangular top of the spine and at the middle. The waist strap was made similarly with a snap hook on one end that attached lower on the spine and clasped in the middle with a 1 inch wide buckle. Once fitted, it slips over the shoulders and buckles at the waist, quick and easy.

The first time trying on the finished Dragon Spine was dreamlike. It's extremely validating to experience one of those rare moments where the reality of your project works just as you had imagined in your head. I could not have been prouder of the outcome. Perhaps I'll make matching dragon wings for it someday.

SPECIAL NOTES

YOU CAN NEVER HAVE ENOUGH CATALOGS. Many companies send a catalog with your first purchase, but you can usually request a catalog for free, or for a reasonable purchase fee.
I have dozens of catalogs full of hardware options that I pore over when I find myself stuck or just to browse the volumes of hardware or notions available… sometimes a previously unknown item can completely change the trajectory of my inspiration.
If you're starting on a project that has unique properties or are stumped in an existing project, spend some time perusing these treasures just waiting for you to discover them- you may find a special kind of buckle with a weird name that does EXACTLY what you were needing, or finally find the hardware piece you needed but had no name for, and so couldn't search for.

The Dragon Spine, complete!

BEAR IN MIND: Every project has different goals, and must be approached differently. Your project should meet your needs. This project was specifically designed to be commercially reproducible. A one-off project for yourself could use a pricier material or rare piece of hardware. Had I been designing just for myself I wouldn't have had to think about adjustability, or the availability of leathers and hardware.

Chapter 14 Cover Model: Laura Meyer
Expert's Corner images courtesy of Luke Milton

Chapter Fifteen

Too Much Fance for Pants
Embellishments and Embroidery
Bonus: Perfect sheer hems

This chapter gets into some nitty-gritty techniques on decorative embellishments, but also practical advice on the tricky feat of getting a lovely narrow hem with sheer fabrics.

I Have A Problem
I don't know if I've ever had a busier autumn.
Because I am physically incapable of uttering the word "No", I was making a line of gowns for the TeslaCon fashion show, in addition to manning a table at the convention to sell my first book. I would also be at a convention in Chicago three weeks before TeslaCon and vending at a convention in New Orleans less than two weeks before TeslaCon. Clearly, I was insane.

However, a decent amount of time to plan out the outfits, and I wasn't making all of them from scratch; a few of the outfits had simply never seen the runway before, and that was good enough for me to include them. Two were ready to go, two needed some revamping before the convention, and two were completely new designs. The two new designs became commissions for some lovely folk who were fans of my work and had always wanted to purchase a gown. These gowns were custom created and fitted for them, and their preferences were taken into account as I designed the dresses.

A Jeweled Gown
One of these gorgeous dresses would utilize a material I had always wanted to use… beetle wings.
Beetle wing embroidery reached the height of its popularity in the Victorian era. The wings are very lightweight and iridescent, glimmering with jewel-like tones of blue and green. They are still in use around the world today, most commonly seen in jewelry. On farms, the wings are harvested from the beetles after they come to the end of their life cycle.

I decided the front panel of the corseted gown would be lined in beetle wings, and they would be used as accents on the long flowing sleeves, at the shoulders and down the back of the skirt. As the wings are also brittle and easily cracked or crushed, I carefully considered the practicality of design in placement of the wings. Placing most of the wings at the

relatively flat and heavily reinforced front of the corseted bodice was intentional- there would be little movement. The beetle wing-adorned "tail" I made for down the back of the gown tied on separately so it could be easily lifted out of the way when the wearer wanted to sit. The wings along the bustline, shoulders and at the base of the split sleeves…. well, you should only be so practical when making a ball gown.

The skirt of the gown had a base metallic fabric, shimmering in the same colors as the wings, and an elegant sheer overskirt to add some mystery to the metallic threads, allowing the wings to take center stage. In fact, this gown debuted on center stage at the TeslaCon Fashion Show in 2022, and there were audible gasps from the audience when the lights hit the gem-like wings.

Delicate Work

It really made the work worthwhile!

And there was a lot of work involved in preparing the wings. They can be purchased in bulk with a hole drilled at the top center of each, or without. I opted for drilled, but I also wanted a hole at the bottom. I would have to do it myself. After some trial and error, I found that an X-acto knife was perfect for the job. I separated the wings into three size categories and got rid of any that seemed too thin or were cracked. Then, one by one, I turned each wing over and place the point of the knife at the center point about a quarter of an inch up from the base and- ever so gently- twisted the knife between my finger and thumb three times, pressing down just enough to drill a hole. I drilled holes in just over 500 wings.

Beyond the preparation, and the fragility of the wings, the actual embroidery was not that much different than embroidering other materials. I've sewn crystals, vintage crystals and pearls onto fabrics and trims, as well as creating jewelry out of the embroidering materials.

The Embroidery

Whether it's pearls, crystals, or beetle wings, I've found two things are particularly important in my embroidery experience. The first is the appropriate size/weight of needle and thread (which pretty much goes for any project) and the other is the use of a backstitch.

In fact, even when stitching metal dragon scales onto a dress panel (as discussed in chapter 5), using a backstitch can help reinforce your sewing, making it less likely that you'll lose your embellishments (or at least, not many), should one be pulled out or should a thread break.

On the bodice of the beetlewing gown, I also used a new length of thread every 6 (or so) wings, so that if one came loose there

wouldn't be a barrage of wings hitting the floor. Besides these precautions, I'm careful not to stitch too tightly. Bunching fabric between embellishments shows up quickly.

Overskirt and sheer hem

This gown was a study in luxurious fabrics; the jewel-like wings, the decadent silk satin of the bodice, the rich metallic shimmer of the under-skirt, and the heer flowing elegance of the long split sleeves and overskirt. Anyone who has worked with a delicate, sheer fabric has also wrestled with it as it stretches, slips, slides and rolls, evading a clean and smooth hem. But after much research (aka fruitless searching online) I combined two techniques to execute an extremely narrow sheer hem… easily. I was astounded. And at that moment, I knew I would find a way to put it into the next book, even if it was more about cosplay and less about sewing.

Yes, that's my segue… it's the end of the book, consider it a bonus tip!

Do You Have the Wing?: The iridescent wings of beetles, particularly those from the jewel beetle family, are prized in embroidery for their vibrant colors and unique texture. Beetle wings can be used to create stunning visual effects, though they require careful handling due to their delicate nature.

- *-Note-* It seemed to me that the beetle wings with a brown hue on their back side tended to be more brittle than others…I sorted them out and only used them if necessary.
- *Get the Good Stuff:* Select high-quality crystals and beetlewings. Lower-quality crystal options may use adhesives instead of prong settings, and leach onto your fabric, very cheap plastic pearls may shed their sheen, and beetlewing may be thin and brittle- ensure they are ethically sourced and properly preserved.
- *Preparation:* Carefully cut beetle wings to the desired size and shape. Use a sharp pair of scissors, and handle them gently to avoid breaking the delicate material. Drill using the tip of an exacto knife; holding the wing in place gently, place the knife where you want the hole and roll it back and forth between your fingers.
- *Storage:* Store embroidered pieces in a cool, dry place away from di-rect sunlight to prevent fading or degradation of materials. Consider using acid-free tissue paper to protect delicate elements. Beetle wings should be stored in such a way as to prevent pressure on the wings.
- *Repairing:* If crystals or beetle wings become loose, carefully reat-tach them using the techniques mentioned. Damaged wings can be replaced without much notice if you used a thread to match your base fabric.

Sparkling like gems in the sunlight!

Perfect Sheer Hems Tips

- *Oui:* My "hack" for a perfect sheer hem uses an approach similar to how French seams are constructed, partially.
- *A Line in the Sand:* Begin by marking your desired hem on your sheer fabric. Stitch along that line for the entire hem.
- *Yes, Press Your Luck:* Turn the hem over on the stitching line and press it. Trim along the hem ⅛". At this point, there is ⅛" of material along your hem, pressed up from the line of stitching.
- *Just Encase:* Now, just turn the hem over to encase the ⅛" in a perfect, narrow hem and stitch. The line of stitching there will keep it from stretching, and the narrowness of the ⅛" band will prevent rollover on curves.

All manner of embellishments can add to your costume:

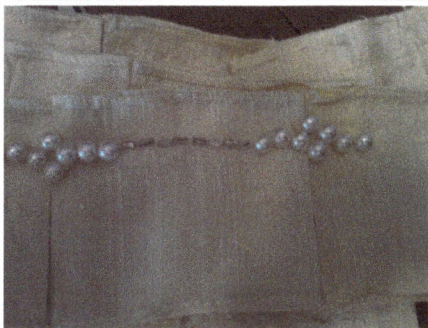

Chapter 15 Beetlewing Gown Model: Kate Peterson
Photographer: Robert Remme

How It's Going:

Photographer: Robert Remme

Laura Meyer believes that life is as much of an event as you make it, and she's here to fance it up. A writer, educator and designer for over two decades, Laura has also spent years teaching, giving presentations and demonstrations on costuming, cosplay, Victorian-era fashion and undergarments, among other topics.

She holds multiple degrees from Alverno College, including a masters in Education. Operating as Twilight Attire since 2001, in 2021 she officially launched Twilight Ember Education Services, LLC, to serve as an umbrella company covering her product lines as well as educational offerings.

Over the last two decades she has hosted and participated in numerous art and fashion shows, flexing her 2D art muscles beyond the usual textile creations. When the boss allows her free time, she enjoys reading, PC gaming, camping, inconsistently dropping blurbs into her blog Repleating History, and giving lots of attention to her furry boy Garrus (without neglecting other, less furry boys).

"The Halloween Collection: Costume & Cosplay Techniques" is her second book. Her first book, "The Victorian Collection: Advanced Costuming Techniques", was printed in 2022 and focused on sewing tips and strategies used in the creation of over a dozen Victorian-inspired gowns. Upcoming printings include the "Cogs Aplenty" steampunk murder mystery game and a cosplay journal, as well as more books across multiple genres in the future!